ARCHIMANDRITE
ARSENIOS KATERELOS

THE JESUS PRAYER
AND ITS APPLICATION

Publisher and Central Distributor :
© Christian Orthodox Philanthropical Society of
Friends of the Pantokrator Sacred Retreat of
Melissohorion "Saint Gregory Palamas"
3, K. Karamanli Street
57200 Liti – Thessaloniki
Phone-Fax : (30) 2394072744
Mobile : (30) 6907364372
URL : www.greekorthodoxbooks.com
Email: info@greekorthodoxbooks.com

© Archimandrite Arsenios Katerelos
Sacred Monastery of Saint Nikolaos
at Divris, Fthiotis, Greece
Phone (+30) 2231094140

English translation from the original Greek text
by Ekaterina Nikolopoulou

Cover design and typesetting
by Gregor Fernbach

First Edition: 2016

ISBN 978-618-81489-4-9

THE JESUS PRAYER AND ITS APPLICATION

THE OPINIONS OF SAINTS, OF ELDER PAISIOS AND OTHER CONTEMPORARY ELDERS

BY ARCHIMANDRITE ARSENIOS
KATERELOS

GREEK ORTHODOX BOOKS

First Edition : 2016

Contents

Foreword

The single-minded Prayer – *«Lord Jesus Christ, have mercy on me»* – is the simplest, but also the most powerful «weapon» of prayer for the faithful – either Monk or layperson. This brief prayer, which was delivered to us by our ancient, holy Fathers of the 6th century, is a condensed form of the entire confession of the Christological Faith of our Church, the complete dogma on the Incarnation of Christ and God, *«in Whose name every knee should bend, of those in heaven and on earth and below the earth»* (Phil.2:10) and with Whose name the powers of perdition are *«flogged»* (Ladder of Divine Ascent, 21:7).

The book titled *«The Jesus Prayer and its application»*, by the respected and beloved Elder, Arsenios Katerelos – a very familiar Spiritual Father, Preacher and author in our Homeland – constitutes an invaluable aid for a Christian's introduction to the art of the precious "Prayer". The Archimandrite Elder Arsenios has deposited the sacred experiences and the teachings of the Elders, Saint Paisios the Hagiorite and Isaac the Lebanese, near whom he had learnt the monk's way of life, enriched with the teaching of the holy Fathers, but also with the discretion that has been based on his own hesychastic experience.

It is with joy that we are delivering this extremely useful guide in the English language, with our prayers that *«the most sweet Jesus*

Christ» will grant the readers of this edition the supernatural delightfulness and benefit of the incessant Prayer.

The Abbott of the Sacred Monastery
"Pantokrator" of Melissohori

† Archimandrite Kyrillos

«The Jesus Prayer and its Application» Prologue to the English Edition

«For just as the Sun is light for the body, thus is prayer for the soul »

(Saint John Chrysostom)

The last instruction of our Lord Jesus Christ – *"Go forth and preach to all the nations..."* (Matth.28:19) - has been applied by the Church since the beginning and until this day, through Her reliable persons, the successors of the Holy Apostles -priests and missionaries- not only directly, by means of their spoken word, but also indirectly, by means of the written and spoken word, with the contribution of technology. Similarly, the translative endeavour of the present essay titled "The Jesus Prayer and its application" into the English language is within the cadre of offering to our distant Orthodox, in-Christ brethren.

As regards direct communication with God, human languages are only a relative thing, given that in essence, that which communicates and becomes united with God through Grace is man's heart, his soul, through which the Holy Spirit *"intercedes in our favour, with ineffable sighs"* (Rom. 8:26) when we receive Him within us – that is," *when the Spirit dwells within us and walks among us* " (2 Cor. 6:16).

We could subsequently say that the chief -and par excellence- language by which we communicate with God is the language of the Holy Spirit. Even so, it is merely a prelude and a foretaste of that which will take place in the future, inasmuch as the language of the future aeon according to Abba Isaac the Syrian will be silence, because then, thanks only to the Grace of the Holy Spirit, there will be full communion with God, but also between mankind, in the land of the living.

As we all know, in our day the languages of the present, deteriorating form of the world -and with the contribution of our weaknesses- are unable to ensure full communion between men, as a result of which, it is never achieved completely in every place and in every age. The Jesus Prayer however is able to bestow the language of the Holy Spirit to man, making it possible for him to converse in silence with God, incessantly, even from this lifetime.

We are therefore expressing our grateful thanks, firstly to the venerable Elder Kyrillos, Abbott of the Sacred Retreat "Pantokrator" of Melissohori, also to the sacred Brotherhood that surrounds him, as well as the Christian Orthodox Philanthropical Society of the friends of the said Retreat, with the name "Saint Gregory Palamas", which is under the shelter of the Very Reverend Abbot; despite the paucity of the text, they have been willing and have condescended to the realization of this translation, for the benefit of a more widespread flock and for the glory of God.

We likewise extend our heartfelt thanks to Ms. Ekaterina Nikolopoulou, who was the translator of the said text. We also pray that the well-intentioned souls of those either close to, or far from, our Orthodox faith - who may thirst for a prayerful communication with God, but are not familiar with the Greek language – will sense and comprehend through the present English translation of the text, that our Orthodox Catholic Church truly experiences the noetic Jesus Prayer within Her bosom; that She truly possesses the prayer of the Pentecost which has been delivered by the Apostles and that She is also responsibly passing it on to Her flock, through Her Saints.

May the blessings of the Holy Fathers accompany all those who have subjected themselves to the labours of translating and publishing, and may the breath of the prayerful Grace of the Jesus Prayer touch, warm and set ablaze the hearts of those who desire the divine delight that comes from the incessant communication through prayer with our Lord and God, Jesus Christ.

In closing, we humbly ask for the blessings and prayers of those who have studied the present essay and have obtained some morsels of spiritual benefit.

Archimandrite Arsenios Katerelos

A FEW WORDS ABOUT FATHER ARSENIOS KATERELOS

Father Arsenios Katerelos had become acquainted with the Blessed Paisios the Hagiorite in the summer of 1979, at the age of 17. From then on he continued to have a close and frequent spiritual contact with him, through to the repose of the Saint in 1994.

When Fr. Arsenios was still a layperson, the Blessed Paisios had recommended Fr. Isaac the Lebanese as his Elder, who resided in the Hut of the Resurrection at Kapsala of the Holy Mountain (and reposed in 1998).

The Elder Isaac was a genuine and very close pupil of the Blessed Paisios, who had also given him the Grand Angelic Schema. The Elder Isaac had abandoned Lebanon for the Blessed Paisios' sake, and had relocated permanently to the Holy Mountain.

During his time at the Holy Mountain (at Kapsala, Panagouda, etc.), Fr. Arsenios was given the opportunity – first as a layperson, later as a novice monk and eventually as a hieromonk – to participate in many Services and Night-vigils with the Blessed Elder Paisios, along with certain other fathers.

Generally speaking, Fr. Arsenios was able to actually hear the teachings of the Blessed Paisios, and was frequently given the opportunity (with the blessing and the exhortation of his Elder, Isaac), to pose various questions to him, on a variety of spiritual topics, both personal and general.

1. INTRODUCTION

The evangelical word of our Lord Jesus Christ which says "***you must always pray and not despair***" (Luke 18:1) – in other words, the fact that we must pray at all times and not give up and be discouraged – is the lifelong experience of our Church's Saints. Furthermore, Saint Gregory the Theologian, who summarizes the value of prayer but also man's stance in his communication with God, would proclaim it dynamically, with one phrase: "Remembrance of God is better than breathing".

It was in the spirit of this instruction by the Lord, as well as the stance and guidance of the Fathers, that we organized a series of evening homilies regarding prayer - the general theme being "The Jesus Prayer". These seven homilies took place in the year 1999 in the holy temple of the Most Holy Lady in the town of Lamia during synaxes of the faithful; they are self-inclusive and consecutive. They were delivered mostly to laypeople, which is why we adjusted the topic appropriately, to suit the spiritual capabilities of the audience. However, these homilies pertain to the entire pleroma – that is, including the clergy and monastics whose main opus is that of prayer. The chronologically last homily which is presented herein as first in line and titled "Elder Paisios and his teaching regarding prayer" took place during a solemn Vespers service in the sacred Metropolitan Temple of the Sacred Metropolis of Fthiotis in the year 2014; we have incorporated it herein, because it is directly linked to our aforementioned topic.

As our beloved readers will discern, we are embarking on a purely practical level as regards the Jesus Prayer, by conveying experiences and opinions mainly of contemporary, blessed Elders. Furthermore, apart from the homilies, we have also included concise replies to the queries of pious attendees. We would like to stress that, albeit a theoretical topic, what is basically presented is the practical consideration of this noble and absolutely necessary labour of prayer – that is, especially of the Noetic Prayer of: "**Lord Jesus Christ, have mercy on me, the sinner**", which is usually recited with the use of a sacred prayer-rope. This "Prayer" – as the specific method of praying is called – is, among other things, a weapon against our three merciless enemies: the Devil, the world afar from God, and -first and foremost- our own, evil self.

However this spiritual weapon is not for exclusive use by monastics, who must dutifully attend to it and apply it as a method and a way of life (as stressed by the Elder Ephraim of the Katounakia region of the Holy Mountain, that "a monk without the mental prayer is not a monk"), but is also at the disposal of all the faithful, according to the teaching of our

Church, which is summarized by the herald of Grace, Saint Gregory Palamas. And it is all the more applicable in our day and age – an age of fatigue, confusion from every aspect, and most of all, of spiritual ignorance.

The Jesus Prayer - both brief and extremely succinct- can be applied, not only ***"in every place of his dominion"*** (Psalm 102:22), but also at any hour of the day or night that the faithful himself desires. As for the results: they are extremely beneficial, as each person who desires to savour that "***Christ is virtuous***" (Psalm 33:9) will see for himself. As we all know, the work of praying cannot be taught; it is revealed to us and is recognized as being "from the Father of lights" wherever there is the proper disposition for struggle, but moreso wherever there is humility, the mother of prayer. However, being humans, it is the teaching and the methodology of the Holy Fathers on the matter which comprise the blessed path that allows the praying person to enter his room and there converse "face to face" with Jesus Himself.

Of course we are not reassured that we have exhausted the overall topic of prayer with these homilies – especially on the noetic Prayer of the heart. On the contrary, we believe that by means of these homilies and these simplified texts we are giving every in-Christ brother who studies them "as a thirsting doe" the opportunity to hasten even more to the "***springs of the waters***" (Psalm 41/42:2), both for a theoretical instruction through the study of Patristic writings on the topic, as well as for the primarily practical application of the most holy and important labour on earth; that is, the work of sacred prayer, and especially of the noetic Prayer.

We are certain of this, not only because the Prayer cultivates and opens horizons within the realm of our mind, rendering our spiritual heart a temple of God, but also because it provides us with the reason to become wiser, in accordance with the quote ***"give a wise man a reason, and he will become wiser"*** (Prov.9:9).

Progress, therefore, in wisdom and in communication with God is attained through the Prayer.

As for us here, it is understood that we invoke the wishes and the prayers of all the readers, so that the Gospel words: ***"but whosoever does and teaches…."*** (Matthew 5:19) may apply to our unworthy person also.
Amen.

On the 6th of June 2014
Archimandrite Arsenios Katerelos

2.
THE ELDER PAISIOS AND HIS TEACHING REGARDING THE PRAYER

Reverend Father and Priest, we shall attempt, in the cadre of your paternal exhortation and with your blessings, to provide certain indications regarding the multi-faceted topic that you asked of our unworthiness. The topic is "The Elder Paisios and his teaching regarding the Prayer".

As such, we shall mention –entirely epigrammatically- certain teachings and events that pertain to the blessed Elder and the topic in question, drawing mainly from personal notes that we had taken at the time, either from Elder Paisios' replies and teachings, or from my Elder, Fr. Isaac the Lebanese Hagiorite… although, most of those notes are indelibly etched inside us.

The Elder frequently used to say that prayer is the soul's oxygen; it is the life of the soul; it is the mirroring of man's spiritual progress and condition. Progress in spiritual matters is unthinkable without a personal improvement in prayer, which is where our spiritual condition can be seen. He would stress selflessness in spiritual living; a thing that naturally reflects in prayer also. Being a true emulator of Christ, his prayer would extend even as far as enemies.

He would say that a Christian has to also embrace those who hate him; to also pray for his crucifiers.

In fact, the Elder himself had at one time prayed with deep pain for God to be merciful even to demons. He pitied them, because he had discerned the demons' "progress" in bestiality, in the host of evil things that they had been striving to outrightly and insidiously inflict on the Elder. In other words, he was pained by the increment of their personal damnation. However, during his prayer he had seen a demon that had transformed into a macabre, bloodthirsty dog's head sarcastically poking its very long tongue out and cynically mocking him...

The Elder used to say that we must constantly be in contact and preparedness for the Celestial Headquarters, like good Army and Heavenly Communications Officers of the Lord. We need to maintain a clear and strong contact with the Heavenly Station. Permit us to call it "Heavenly Internet" or "Divine-net". To achieve this, it is imperative – according to the Elder always – that the powers of our soul execute their "chores", their "handiwork" diligently (these were the Elder's words); in other words, their potentials – the ones given to us by God.

When the Elder was once asked: "Should we approach God using logic or the heart?" he replied with a simple, representative and wise word: "To locate and listen to a radio station we need to suitably adjust two buttons: the radio's frequency and the volume. The volume is logic and the frequency is the heart." In other words, both are necessary – at least at the beginning.

In another context, when the Elder had embarked on a deeper discussion, he told us among other things that: "The noblest thing that the good Lord gave man is the mind – the 'nous' – the 'holy trinity of our soul'. Because God only reveals Himself to the nous, where God's uncreated energy unites with the essence of our nous and obviously with the Prayer; after the solidified 'spiritual lubricant' has softened, then all of the above are activated, with everything that this entails. The practical consequence of the aforementioned is the fine-tuning of our 'receiver' towards humility."

With these words, the Elder implied that this was the only way to attain an ontological, existential and live replenishment between us and God. The Elder never isolated the Prayer from the rest of his spiritual life. In certain cases, he would even stress that: "What we need here is more attention and less prayer." He placed a huge importance on one's humble mien and on proper thoughts. He would say: "A thought can 'block' or 'unblock' the Prayer; when we don't forgive or ask for forgiveness, our prayer not only doesn't fly up to Heaven, it doesn't even rise above our own head." He said this metaphorically of course...

He obviously didn't regard the Prayer as an end in itself, but rather, a necessary and perpetual means – together with other forms of ascesis – for the discarding of the old self and for our union with God. He used to say something along the lines of: "We should be contemplating God's infinite benefactions, and our innumerable –known and unknown– sins, our omissions etc. These will all generate humility inside us; a salvific cardiac pain, and thus, the Prayer will not be a conventional and tiresome thing; it will instead become a personal, natural need for the invocation of divine mercy, but also for glorification."

He regarded this as far superior to the application of various praying techniques such as special breathing, the use of stools, etc. He of course had respect for all these techniques, but regarded them as mere aids that would help the nous to concentrate on the Prayer. In parallel, he would not omit to point out various physical and spiritual dangers (such as imagining that we are doing something lofty), but would also point out the organic dangers that can arise, such as heart problems on account of the pressure exerted by the flesh.

He would often say that, before counting knots on our prayer ropes, we should instead count our innumerable sins or read a patristic text in order to attain awareness, thus escaping from mundane things and focusing only on the words of the Prayer; that we should also ignore all of our musings without exception – the personal ones, the impassioned ones, the demonic ones, those "from the left", those "from the right", the beneficial ones, the blasphemous ones etc…

He would stress the following: "We mustn't be surprised (especially during prayers) that the enemy doesn't rest. We can actually exploit him", he used to say, "by making him an unpaid laborer who will actually prod us to persist in the incessant Prayer." To clarify this comment, he told us of a spiritual struggler, who, when lying down to sleep would be besieged by demons that gave him unclean thoughts. To which he reacted by exclaiming: "It's a good thing that you reminded me!" and would then get up and perform many prostrations… The Elder had commented that when we have a conscience like that man's, then the little urchin isn't a fool: when it scopes out (he would say this quite often) that it will lose the battle, it knows it is not to its advantage to persist (and thus work for free), because instead of causing us harm it is actually doing us good.

The Elder placed great importance on one's thoughts and one's proper, healthy conscience, as well as on our proper spiritual placement opposite God, our fellow-man, etc.. "This is where we have a serious 'oil leakage', he would say, "which is why unfortunately there are no spiritual fruits."

He would stress that we should ask only for divine mercy in our prayers, in order to repent in a proper manner that is pleasing to God, and thus be forgiven so that we might see our wretched state, much more clearly and in depth. "Only thus," he would say, "will God give you His grace, my blessed child, and whatever else is necessary for your salvation and your fellow man's." "Unless we come to abhor ourselves God-wise (without a trace of despair), we shall continue to tumble into new pitfalls - both latent and evident ones. This spiritual state naturally varies, from the novice to the perfected, given that it is a progress that never ends.

This contemporary holy father used to say: "I'm only a tin can; just because sunlight is reflected off it sometimes, you think that I am the sun." Other times he would say (and mean it, 100%): "I am just an unplated tin can".

He would also say of a certain monk who was admittedly quite ascetic and of good repute: "All his prayer-ropes are useless..." The Elder must have "seen" something negative in him... which is why he often stressed that we shouldn't perform a dry, tasteless ascesis, aspiring to (obviously or secretly) attain divine experiences, illumination, gifts, prophecies etc.. There are those, he would say, who increase their prayer-ropes while observing an external, formal precision in various rubrics (without the rubrics being to blame of course – quite the contrary), in their futile belief that they are faithfully observing the Philokalian texts. In a nutshell, they are only censing, projecting and sanctifying themselves. Should they encounter the praise of the faithful, the innocent, the naïve, the pseudo-pious, the inexperienced, the fanciful, the psychopaths, the cunning, the opportunist, the self-serving etc., then things become extremely dangerous from every aspect, as well as uncontrollable and unfortunately, most of the time almost incurable. This is because the "little urchin" exploits them, invisibly, with cunning mastery, and gives them what he called "urchinist" experiences, impressions and self-deceptions, supposed prophecies, coincidences, delusions upon delusions, of which there is no number…

He would say that in spite of its difficulties, a God-pleasing prayer relaxes and creates an ineffable peace inside us. It's shameful - he used to say - when Christ Himself offers us the potential to communicate with Him, for us not to be willing to – or, not to have the analogous awareness during such a communication. On the one hand we envy and regard as blessed those who lived during Christ's time and were able to speak to Him, instead of stopping to think that we are in a far more advantageous situation - inasmuch as we are able to be in a continuous contact with Him, spiritually… In Christ's time, people weren't able to secure His personal attention very easily (vying as to who could be first in line to preoccupy Him) etc..

The Elder not only stressed the quality of prayer, but also the quantity. When the latter is observed in the proper manner, the former is improved as well. He himself would naturally pray for hours on end, for endless nights and days. But what am I saying? The Elder obviously possessed the cardiac, effortless, self-acting noetic Prayer, during his sleep but also while awake, whether talking or whatever else he was preoccupied with. This of course was the fitting, God-sent fruit and gift that gave the Elder his many, personal spiritual parameters, struggles and "promotive" temptations.

He was so dedicated to praying that – for example – when living as an ascetic at Sinai, away from the Monastery, all alone, young at the time and relatively unknown and obscure, he would go to the Monastery every now and then – that is, every fifteen days – for the sole purpose of receiving Holy Communion, and no other reason. One time –and only that one time- he underwent inconceivable tortures by the cunning one. He used to say "I felt as though I was nailed to the Cross". Of course one can comprehend this statement, not when simply hearing it, but only when it is actually experienced, and to the degree it was experienced.

Among other things, we humbly believe is it permissible for us to mention that the devil was the one prompting him to go to the Monastery – imagine, the devil prompting one to go to the monastery (!!) and attend services etc with the other fathers – in other words, in order to abandon his solitude. It was a move that the devil had preferred for a reason. At the time, Fr. Paisios had also braved various human pressures, even by spiritual persons... but let's not say anything more on this. (After all, it wasn't the sole instance at the time and only on that topic; there had been other instances and for other reasons, both earlier and later...) Anyway, the Elder had bravely resisted that will of the devil. But when he received Holy Communion at the Monastery after fifteen days, he savoured the Holy Communion as sweet-tasting meat – and not only that; he was filled with a divine sweetness: that of the Uncreated Light. Thus, with renewed spiritual powers and heavenly experiences, he would provoke (not the people of course - the Elder would never provoke people – only the devil) for the following fifteen days during his solitary ascesis, and would himself prod the devil, saying: "If you want, come on, let's fight again!" Naturally, he was boasting in the Lord. And he was of course implying –among other things – that he wouldn't allow anything to disturb his solitude, whatever that entailed. We need to make a necessary clarification here: What he did was possible, only thanks to the Elder's spiritual measures. After all, he had also frequently stressed the value of common prayer. He used to say: "The temple is God's house. Praying alone is one's preparation for the common prayer." To be sure, common prayer does have distractions etc., therefore at times it may be somewhat inferior; it is, however, more powerful – both because of the unity (very important, but we won't analyze it here), as well as of the number of those praying.

Dear brethren, quite frequently, when one has been observing his penance properly in his cell, but without God giving him any tangible "taste" of Grace, he may sometimes in church –entirely effortlessly and easily – be actually unable to stop the excessively sensuous waves of Grace... the Uncreated "divine rain"... The instances are of course innumerable and the topic requires special examination.

It is needless to mention that the Elder placed the utmost significance in one's participation in sacramental ecclesiastic life - its highlight of course being the proper reception of Holy Communion.

One time, when receiving Holy Communion in one of the cells on the Holy Mountain where the Elder felt cold on account of the lack of heating, his age, and the various ailments that he suffered from, he quite suddenly and entirely supernaturally felt warmed after Holy Communion, both spiritually and bodily – so much so, that on his return to his Cell, even the path he walked on had warmed up! Such a "squandering" of thermo-divine energy...

The Elder strongly believed in the power and the benefit of prayer, which is why he would often humbly and systematically avoid contact with people, even for long periods of time. When at Sinai, he would even put up "danger" signs painted with skulls; his intention was to make visitors think that the area was a minefield and therefore too dangerous to approach.

He was also very glib and witty, with an instinctive, beneficial sense of humour and a very dynamic and vivid character.

For example, a visitor to the Holy Mountain went to the Elder's cottage and rang the bell for him to open. After a long wait, the Elder opened the door and said: "Hey there, what do you want, young man?" "I wanted to see you, Elder", he replied. "Well, didn't you just see me? Would you also like me to do an about-face so you can see me better?" The visitor was taken aback, then, with a certain dose of anxiety, he said: "I would like you to pray for me, Elder". And the Elder replied jokingly: "Go away so I can pray. If you don't leave, how am I going to pray?"

To another visitor who worried that war was going to break out, the Elder said: "Don't be afraid, they haven't recalled any ambassadors yet" (meaning the ambassadors of the countries involved). Then, jokingly, he continued: "If a recall of mediators does occur, only then should we say 'With the mediations of the Theotokos, o Saviour, save us'." The Elder was obviously utilizing a play on words wisely and beneficially, while also implying at the time that no war was imminent.

Needless to say that –especially at the Elder's cottage at Panagouda- the crowds who went there for his counsel had greatly increased. Very often the Elder – with his truly God-given insight, which he never "gave away" unnecessarily – knew when to open or not, and when to speak extensively or succinctly, and he would naturally hide this gift very artfully. There have been very few instances where he had revealed it very faintly- and with a ready alibi. It would usually be because of his love, or if he was mainly "pressured" by God to reveal it.

One time, a pious lady who encountered him in "the world" said to him: "Elder, I constantly invoke you in your Cell on the Holy Mountain. Could you hear me?" To which he replied very plainly and with humour: "Why? Did you think I was deaf?"

Despite his strictly observed spiritual measures he was afraid (because of the multitudes of pilgrims) of losing the submersion of his nous in extended prayer, where time-space stands still and is lost.

As he used to say, "If the nous is dulcified inside the heart, it has no desire of departing from there." In other words, to rephrase it more theologically, he meant the return of the nous' energy to the nous' essence. In this blissful state the nous stands still because of the tangible and excessive, hedonic divine Grace. At times, all contact with the environment is lost, and prayer essentially ceases. Divine Grace "transports" you wherever it wants, without asking you. Albeit a "divine constraint", it is, nevertheless, the product of an ideal and proper, godly use of our self-government.

However, there were two celestial events that we know of, which exhorted the Elder to thereafter to receive pilgrims. The one time (the second one that we are aware of), his own blessed Elder, Father Tychon the Russian appeared to him from heaven, ringing his doorbell like a terrestrial visitor. He said in a heavenly voice: "I'm glad that you're receiving people". The first time that Father Tychon had appeared to him – always from heaven – was on the 10/9/1971. Of course there was another time too, but beware: that time it was the devil who took on the form of Father Tychon in order to mislead him, but the Elder Paisios had his wits about him...

The second event was when the Elder was instructed by the Holy Mother Herself to receive visitors...

As a basic prayer rule he proposed the prayer rope for monks in their cell, but not only for cell-dwellers and not only for monks. To get a small "taste", we will mention certain related numbers per "usage", as follows:

Initially, four "crossed" 300-knot prayer ropes, that is, with small prostrations – three to Christ, saying "Lord Jesus Christ have mercy on me" and the fourth to the Holy Mother, saying "Most holy Theotokos, save me".

Additionally, four "free" prayer ropes, that is, with or without making the sign of the Cross, as above, for ourselves. "Lord Jesus Christ, have mercy on me" and "Most holy Theotokos, save me".

Also, four more "free" (always 300-knot) prayer ropes for the living, saying with the first three "Lord Jesus Christ have mercy on us" and one "Most holy Theotokos, save us".

Then another four (300-knot) prayer ropes for the deceased, of which the first three with "Lord Jesus Christ, repose Thy servants" and the fourth to the Holy Mother, with "Most holy Theotokos, repose Thy servants". Finally, a 300-knot prayer rope to the Saints of each day. "Saints of God, mediate for us". In other words, 17 prayer ropes (of 300 knots) on a daily-nightly basis and many, many others, and other methods etc, which are not possible to mention at this time.

He was especially concerned about not saying the Prayer quickly, so that we might fully absorb it, and in general (a detail that concerns us) the analogy of time dedicated to Christ and the Theotokos, which, according to the Elder should always be three to one (3:1), without this being absolute or compulsory. He of course recommended many "deep" prostrations (head touching the floor). He also told us of a certain monk who sometimes actually saw the Saints of the day, both the familiar and the unfamiliar ones.

The chapter "Elder Paisios – the Prayer" is obviously an inexhaustible one. The Elder left behind a great many things; and yet, he took with him incomparably more, inasmuch as we would have been unable to interpret them – assuming he would have been more revealing…

Once, when someone asked him about the Uncreated Light, the Elder (albeit "swimming" in it very many times himself) replied: "How should I know what that is? The stove that I have in my cell is certainly a created item!" He was referring to the Rumanian/ Russian stoves that were built with firebricks.

Finally, the Elder used to say: "When you feel grief, you're lacking something". That is why we beseech you, Reverend, who have so often in practice and over Time expressed your respect for the hallowed figure of Elder Paisios - as evident in the 2011 Calendar of the Sacred Metropolis of Fthiotis and in so many more ways – we beseech you to pray that this truly hallowed Elder bestows on each of us from the heavens the "spiritual vitamins" that we lack. That way, we shall all enter more and more deeply into a more Orthodox, personal spiritual orbit, which will stave off the sorrow of our sin and give us the peace of God, which are far above every nous.

Amen.
May it be so!
With your blessings.
I thank you.

3.
INTRODUCTORY HOMILY ON THE PRAYER

By the Grace of God and the Most Reverend Father's paternal blessing and exhortation for a combined pastoral, catechist, confessional and liturgical opus, we will embark on our first introduction today, my reverent fathers and my beloved in-Christ brethren.

Naturally, being fully aware of every kind of weakness, we would undoubtedly prefer silence. Which is why –to the extent that it depends on us– we have allowed ourselves to preach in our Monastery very seldom, as we always prefer to be disciples of the Saints – that is, to those who have lived a life in spiritual theory.

That is the reason why most times – especially during night-vigils – we prefer readings taken from Patristic texts: it is because whatever the Saints ever said and wrote wasn't done "encyclopedically" – intellectually – the way we do today... we take from here, we take from there, we borrow from there... and so we should, because it's safer... but, what did all the predecessors (mainly Saints) used to say, primarily and above all else? They spoke only of things that they had personally experienced – only whatever had been a personal achievement. In general, they learnt the divine things and they taught what they had learnt, only after having experienced them. That is why their word has a particular impact.

This explains the phenomenon whereby they who were blessed by God to become acquainted with holy people, were able to keep their counsels and their words alive in their memory, as though these were given just yesterday – even if they who had spoken to them were illiterate or without any charisma or trained in elocution, or with a tenuous voice or stammerers, or unfamiliar with the rules of rhetoric etc. On the contrary, certain homilies by trained orators may temporarily sound pleasing, but in the end they will not have the analogous power to shake us and convince us, the way that the former can, whose words originate from the excess of their heart, unassumingly and instinctively; Above all, they spoke from personal experience and were not theorizing.

This explains how I, the lowly one, was able to remember in every detail my first conversation with the blessed Elder Paisios the Hagiorite twenty years ago, at the age of 16-17. We were High School students at the time, and we hadn't gone there with a disposition to benefit; it was merely out of curiosity. Even when the Elder asked us "Do you have a spiritual guide?" and "Does he give you repose?" we – a group of three – exchanged looks between us and asked ourselves what the Elder meant, "if the spiritual guide reposes us", because we didn't have a clue what those words meant, even though we had gone to Confession several times. The Elder realized that we were quite clueless with regard to spiritual matters. He then said to us – pained and lovingly – "You obviously haven't savoured any spiritual joys... I pray that you will attain them, and (as he used to say to many others)- that you will attain the beneficial "spiritual restlessness" so that later on you will also attain spiritual joys."

Well, Fr. Paisios was the first person to shake us spiritually – without being asked by us of course – and who convinced us more than anyone else ever had, for which we owe him unlimited and perpetual gratitude. Despite our ignorance at the time, he had convinced us of many things. First of all, we came to understand that he was in a hurry to "depart", out of divine love: he fervently longed to go to God. He desired death like it was life. We could discern it, in his entire being, without us making any effort. It was more than obvious, and it permeated all of the actions of the blessed Elder Paisios.

He had also told us various other things, but now is not the time to discuss them. When we departed from there – it was the summer of '79, the month of July – we began to savour our first spiritual joy, without having asked for it, and without being nostalgic for it, because we didn't even know what it meant. We felt an inexplicable joy on leaving his Cell – a joy that accompanied us for several hours - although we had no idea at the time where it had come from. It was, of course, the result of the blessed Elder's prayers, in spite of our unworthiness.

However, even before going to the blessed Elder Paisios, on the previous evening we had met the doorman of the Sacred Monastery of Koutloumousion, the monk (at the time) Arsenios, together with whom I also came to recall the entire conversation. Among other things, Fr.Arsenios had recommended that we find and buy the book "An Ascetic Bishop" by Saint Nephon, Bishop of Constantiane; it was a book whose title we hadn't even heard of at the time.

He told us things that pierced our heart. He also said the following, with regard to spiritual books: "If you read a book once and then you don't need to read it again from time to time, then it wasn't worth reading the first time, my children, because that book lacked the Grace of the Holy Spirit, and therefore would not have lasted throughout eternity – it was not beneficial to the soul."

He was an Agriculturist, and as such, gave various related lessons at the Athonias School; in fact, most of the time he shortened the lesson, not out of indifference, but simply because he could deliver it more concisely because he possessed the skill of a teacher as well as spirituality. He chose to shorten the lesson, because he judged that it would be far more beneficial for them (having gained extra time) to teach them a little about the Jesus Prayer – that is, the "Lord Jesus Christ, have mercy on me".

Of course he did this out of pain and profound love for the children; because, whoever has savoured God's love, cannot stand to see others remain ignorant of it and will strive in every possible way to familiarize them, depending on their place in society: if he is a layperson, or a monk, or a missionary - regardless who he is. The end result is that, one way or another, he will strive to see how he can help any fellow-man spiritually and entirely selflessly, because wherever there is self-seeking, God is not there.

On this matter of teaching, the marvelous Saint Isaac the Syrian says that the virtue which is taught without first having been experienced, resembles the water of a beautifully painted lake in a respective, amazingly painted picture. However, that water, as enticing as it may look, is not actual water but only a depiction of it, and cannot quench the thirst of the onlooker. And he is not only unable to quench his thirst, but, the more beautifully it is painted, in our humble opinion, the more it will arouse and magnify the already existent thirst; that is, it will create an even bigger problem, a greater spiritual void, disappointment, and all other related reactions, if the teacher doesn't have any experience and doesn't put into practice the things that he teaches.

In other words, a virtue that is taught without corresponding praxis and personal experience, not only does NOT benefit – it often even scandalizes; whereas, even if no homily is delivered by one who possesses virtue, a silent spiritual voice will emanate from him in every direction – which is far more beneficial and useful. This is also how the phenomenon of silent teaching mentioned in Patristic literature is explained.

When Saint Anthony the Great was compelled to abandon his ascetic residence – that is, when he judged it to be expedient to go to Alexandria and help the persecuted and suffering Christians there, then, as testified by the ecclesiastic historical authors, with the sight alone of Saint Anthony's countenance and his mien, more people had come to believe in Christ than all those who had come to believe in Him over a significant period of time with the excellent and God-pleasing sermons by other saints – by missionaries – who even possessed all the proper spiritual qualifications and all the Holy-Spiritual prerequisites.

One of the best and most drastic sermons that had ever "struck" me and shaken me in my entire lifetime, from when I was a layperson and which still retains a much respected status among my spiritual experiences, was, finally, neither a sermon nor a homily, but the sight alone of a monk's countenance, who is still alive today.

When I had gone to visit him, that monk was busy clearing weeds, carefree, at a far corner of the plot of land by his Cell; however, I noticed something about him that I never expected. I could not have imagined he would be in a "far out" state – that is, in a state "beyond himself" - but it looked as though he was totally unaware of it too – and of course I was struck by a beneficial spiritual shock. So much was I fascinated by that incredible and indescribable luminance of his body and more so of his face, that I was lost for words. Of course he - acting as though nothing had transpired - simply exhorted me to eat with him, and to even accept three-four sweets... We may be acquaintances, however despite the years that have passed I have never considered, nor dared, to mention that incident to him. I am almost certain that he had undergone many such experiences and situations, and that he probably doesn't know which of them to remember... although, I can't be sure myself, if that monk was indeed aware of what I had witnessed, or if he himself had perceived it at that moment.

Of course what I'm telling you now I could never have imagined at the time; anyway, the matter of how the sighting of the Divine Light is possible, in what ways, in which cases, and how that divine Light can also be reflected on the rest of logical and a-logical Creation is another chapter altogether, which requires a series of homilies.

That monk was a direct reminder of the God-sighting Moses, who, upon receiving the Ten Commandments on Mount Sinai's holy summit, acquired such a radiant countenance that no-one could look directly at his face. Or, perhaps, that monk had given us a first (external, always) "taste" of how Christ must have appeared during His Transfiguration, when His countenance had shone like the Sun and His garments had also become as white as snow, hence His three chief Disciples prostrating themselves in amazement on the ground, *"unable to gaze upon that unimaginable"* brightness of Christ – upon the brightness and the intensity of the divine Light... their earthen hearts being unable to bear that divine experience as the hymnographer says, *"in case they lose their life along with their eyesight"* – in other words, that the sighting of the divine Light might kill them... Although, at the time, Christ had revealed only a small degree of His divinity and not the fullness of it (because the fullness cannot be measured and cannot be revealed to any logical creature – not only now, but even unto the ages of the ages - because it entails an infinity of spiritual dimensions).

Anyway, that monk in general reminds one convincingly of all the (inner) transformations during the theopties (God-sightings) – that many spiritual strugglers have experienced throughout the course of ecclesiastic history. Above all, it convinces and reassures one of that which all the Saints, including Saint Simeon the New Theologian, say: that the Holy Spirit is the same, both in the past, the present and the future, and as the Bible also says, ***"Christ is the same, both yesterday and today"***. In other words, God always wants to give everyone these spiritual states, except that the problem lies in all of us modern Christians and not in God, Who is eternally non-discriminatory. Discrimination does not exist in God.

As in the case of the blessed Saint Sisoe – that bloom of the desert whom we commemorate in July: when his end had neared, his face became bright and it was perceived by those who were present; even so, he kept beseeching God to not take him, but instead allow him to live a little longer to grieve some more and to repent; he was certain that he needed to… begin to repent! When some of them remarked "What could you possibly do in repentance, now that you are an elderly man?" he replied "I can sigh, and that should suffice for me". Now THAT'S Orthodoxy! To be so near to God, and yet truly feel that you haven't even begun to repent!

And to speak more theologically, that monk gave us an outward reassurance as to what our Orthodoxy is and proclaims – that is, that man CAN partake of God's "uncreated energies" : that man can actually "swim" in His divine Grace, as Saint Gregory Palamas used to say during the famous Hesychast disputes - when the essence of genuine, perennial, Orthodox spirituality with Saint Gregory Palamas and several others had collided with the pseudo-spirituality of the Westerners, whose representatives were Barlaam the Calabrian, Gregoras, and some others, who had aspired to altering the "once delivered" Orthodox spirituality.

As Saint Gregory used to say, we cannot reach God by means of cogitations or dialectics - only through actual experience. Reasonings are not enough. God is above reasonings. He is beyond all the forms and the representations of the world. However, we can reach God through experience and theopty (the sighting of God). This theopty is of course form-less and has nothing to do with the assorted pseudo-visions of various individuals, which are either the product of self-suggestion, or fantasy, or psychopathy, or even a camouflaged demonic energy.

And now, let's say something about the in-God "amalgamation", which is about becoming amalgamated (joined) with God. Or, as Saint John of the Ladder says, "to attain congress... with God!" What realism! What boldness! We would never dare utter something like that today! We would most certainly be misunderstood. The Saint says that "congress" implies a personal union with God, in every spiritual and empirical dimension – not in any intellectual or sentimental one, but in actual experiences, which is what man acquires when he partakes of the Grace of God. It is a union, a meeting with God. What amazing words!

I am certain that the sight of this monk (in the state that Divine Providence had allowed us to "catch" him unexpectedly) surpasses every kind of beauty of the present life, whether a legal, or a sinful or an illegal beauty…

So, my dear brethren, I have heeded the invitation by the Very Reverend Father to come here, even though it would have been appropriate for me to remain in the Monastery to grieve as long as necessary (given that the meaning of "monasticism" is about a monk grieving for his sins and praying for the entire world). That's what genuine Orthodox monasticism is; and, if observed properly, its offer is extremely precious.

However, entirely spontaneously, I am reminded of Saint Gregory the Theologian's stance, who, albeit having sublime experiences, nevertheless always avoided administrational cares and responsibilities – even if they happened to be ecclesiastic ones. As Saint Gregory the Theologian used to say: "More important for me is inaction". In other words, more important for him was an "in-God inaction", consisting only of study and prayer... an "inaction" which is the product and a coordinate of many spiritual factors, but now is not the time to discuss and analyze what in-God inaction and quietude are.

However, that which must not escape our attention is that Saints like Gregory the Theologian and Maximos – and not only them – were the bastions of Orthodoxy during extremely difficult periods; or, more correctly, it was persons like these that divine Providence had chosen and utilized, for the good of our Church.

When Basil the Great -as Saint Gregory's friend- had mediated for him to become Bishop of Sasima, Saint Gregory became very upset... among other things, he had made a remark (that we shouldn't rush to misinterpret). He said "I have ceased to believe in friendship". What he implied was that his true friend – Saint Basil the Great – had "done the worst possible spiritual thing" to him, when mediating for him to undertake the responsibility of Bishop. This was the reason that Saint Gregory had departed for Pontus...

There was a period in Saint Gregory the Theologian's time, when all the temples in Constantinople had been taken over by the Arians. Then, in order to escape from their impasse, the few remaining Orthodox had invited Gregory to Constantinople. However, when they saw him in such a haggard and weak state from intensive ascesis, even they who had invited him were disappointed at first glance. They wondered to themselves "This is the one who will save us?"

Furthermore, inasmuch as there was no available Orthodox temple, a rough shack had been constructed, which was named "Saint Anastasia". Then, when Saint Gregory began to deliver his Spirit-bearing homilies (his five Theological Homilies are well-known), things began to change. The Orthodox were charmed thereafter, and the truth of the Triune God, Orthodoxy, eventually prevailed.

When first delivering sermons at Saint Anastasia, he used to say among other things: "These heretics – the Arians – let them have their houses – the temples; if proper worship isn't observed inside them, the temples alone will not save anyone. Let us Orthodox keep the Truth; let us keep the Tenant." Who did he mean by "Tenant"? Of course he meant Christ. When - after several years - he had succeeded in making all of the churches Orthodox and a certain temptation arose (we won't get into that now and digress from the subject), he took the responsibility upon himself – embittered of course as a human – and had asked himself: "Was this turmoil because of me – on my account?" At that moment he was reminded of the Prophet Jonah who was thrown into the sea (Jonah 1:10-16) because of the same suspicion, which is why Saint Gregory finally said to the (now Orthodox) Christians of Constantinople: "Listen. When I first came here, there was no Orthodox Church. Now, with the Grace of God, there is no Arian church. For this, my beloved brethren, I would like you to reward me. And the reward that I would like you to give me is to.... allow me to leave, so I can return to my solitude." You can of course imagine what ensued after that statement...

Saint Isaac the Syrian did something along the same lines, who, as Bishop of Nineveh, remained in his bishopric one or two days at the most. When he saw two Christians quarrelling because the one owed money to the other and the lender (who was demanding his money back in an improper manner from a poor individual who was unable to pay him back), he asked Saint Isaac: "So, what does the Gospel say in this case?" A while earlier, Saint Isaac had said to him "But, my brother, the Gospel says this...and this...as you must know..." When Saint Isaac realized that they didn't pay attention to what the Gospel advised, he remarked: "They didn't respect the Gospel – did you think they would respect me?" Immediately after that – prompted by divine Grace of course and illumined by it – he returned to the desert and his beloved solitude.

So, if a Saint like Gregory had need of solitude and regarded it more important, and if Saint Isaac –who had benefitted so many people solely with his writings over Time– and if all of the aforementioned had, in one way or another proved to be instruments of divine Providence and had saved Orthodoxy, yet had need of solitude, then what should all of us say, who so foolishly believe sometimes that the world has need of us?... Saint Seraphim of Sarov, who had remained a recluse for a considerable length of time, had done something analogous.

However it wasn't only the saints of the past; it was also your own, familiar Father Paisios, which is why I mention him so frequently. At a younger age, when living ascetically as a monk at Sinai (he too was a Sinaite – outside the sacred Monastery of Saint Katherine of course, at Saint Episteme), he used to place various obstacles on the path leading to his Cell. He would place skulls and various bones etc., so that passers-by, mountaineers, tourists etc would believe that the territory there was dangerous, thus deterring them from disturbing him for no reason. Quite often, he would scarcely attend church services at the Monastery's Catholicon (the main temple). This of course by no means applies to us, so we mustn't let it influence us. He sometimes even preferred quietude to the synaxis of the Liturgy… but again, that applied only to Fr.Paisios and to those with the same spiritual measures as his.

On this matter, the blessed Elder used to say: "If you have a nice potato and eat it, the benefit is minimal – you merely ate a potato. But, if you bury that potato for a period of time in the ground – with all the proper agricultural prerequisites of course – then, after a while, you will have many potatoes." What did he imply with that charming example? That if someone were to withdraw, to "bury" himself in quietude (in the Lord) for isolation and ascesis, with the proper conscience of course (because nothing in the Church is an end in itself), by NO means will it be damaging, but will in fact be greatly beneficial, both personally as well as communally – that is, for the entire pleroma of our Holy Church.

We are here today in order to deposit the experience of many holy men whom we had encountered on the path of our wretched life, according to the quote "I am not a monk, and as such, a Christian, but I have seen actual Christian monks".

Now, these have just been introductory words. I would like to inform you at this point that during the first lessons of our synaxes we will focus on a "hot", practical and extremely beneficial topic – the succinct prayer of: "Lord Jesus Christ, have mercy on me the sinner" or, more simply, "Lord Jesus Christ, have mercy on me".

We will mention and prove that this prayer is not merely an exhortation by our holy Church but rather a commandment, inasmuch as it is included in the more general commandment regarding prayer - that is, the familiar "pray incessantly" – and that it does not pertain only to monks, but to all the laity, to every Christian.

That certain people believe the opposite is a huge mistake. Throughout the passage of History -and in our time- there have been Christians who are intently focused on the Prayer and have witnessed many spiritual fruits.

The words "pray incessantly" are a commandment; they are not a needless luxury, and they are for all Christians. And let no-one think that the struggles of the laity have many differences compared to those of monastics. Of course the monastic isolates himself and vows virginity, undoubtedly, and there is also the specialized obedience to his spiritual Elder whom he has freely chosen beforehand, and to the renunciation of possessions. Woe betide the monk who has property, and the monk who boasts inwardly about possessing a fortune, or one who is concerned with and desires to perform many acts of charity. The most important thing for monastics is the renunciation of all material possessions.

We shall further examine what the stages of the Prayer are; that we should initially recite it in a whispering voice, then mentally, and then from the heart. We shall also examine the following: What the method of the Prayer is; what additional advantages this prayer has, compared to other prayers of our holy Church. Naturally all prayers originate from the Holy Spirit. Psalmody is necessary, and praying is necessary, and the noetic Prayer is necessary. We shall therefore explain what temptations it confronts, what difficulties, what inexpressible joys, and finally, everything else that pertains to the Prayer.

Of course we must never forget that these homilies are mainly addressed to laypeople and that we shall be as discreet as we possibly can on this detail.

That was all we had to say for today, purely as an introduction. Next Saturday, at the same time and here, in the holy temple of the All-holy Mother, we shall embark on the first homily on the Jesus Prayer.

4.
PREREQUISITES AND BENEFITS OF THE PRAYER

As announced during our first synaxis, my beloved, in-Christ brethren, as of today we shall be discussing the Prayer, and especially about an (unfortunately forgotten) way of praying. It is about the Jesus Prayer: the "Lord Jesus Christ, Son of God, have mercy on me the sinner", or, more concisely, more succinctly: "Lord Jesus Christ, have mercy on me".

However, before examining this simple albeit most drastic manner of praying, we deem it absolutely essential to say a few introductory words on praying, which we must have an elementary knowledge of, so that we can maximize the multiple and multi-faceted benefit that will come, especially from the Jesus Prayer.

For man, praying is a privilege. And praying involves our being elevated towards heaven, as well as dialogue and personal communication with God. As for its quality, it is about becoming "conjoined" to God - to His Uncreated Energies.

But we must not forget that praying is one of the commandments – one of the more basic ones. With prayer we improve in the observation of the commandments. But also inversely, by observing the commandments we progress in prayer. Prayer reflects our overall spiritual course; and, in order for it to be welcomed by God, it is absolutely necessary that we observe certain prerequisites as best we can. Otherwise, if they aren't observed, our prayer not only won't reach heaven or be acceptable to God; it won't even be elevated above our head – metaphorically speaking of course. As Fr. Paisios used to say so charmingly, "it won't even surpass the height of our own head".

Elder Paisios once said to someone: "With the routine that you're following, your prayer not only doesn't reach the sky; it in fact remains – height wise – even below your own head." The Elder had said something analogous to someone who didn't recite the Prayer "correctly", but instead in a rather inappropriate manner – not calmly and soberly, in order to "assimilate" the Prayer. He recited it with a mania – not in God's way, but in an unnatural manner – a manner that caused anxiety and created a not-so-spiritual style... That person wouldn't even say "bless me" when greeting those he'd encounter on the street, for fear of losing the Prayer – which he would recite out loud, very loud, in a manner that was... well.... not so appropriate. So, when Fr. Paisios asked him, out of love of course (that person was a novice monk at the time): "What are you doing there, brother?" he replied: "Elder, I am saying 'the Prayer'." "What 'Prayer', blessed child? Is that the way to say 'the Prayer'? The way you're doing it, take care you don't become demon possessed", Fr Paisios replied, then counseled him on certain details.

We therefore need to be careful while praying extensively, in case for some reason our prayer doesn't fly upwards to heaven.

The prerequisites of prayer are inexhaustible, but some of them are the following:

First of all, our prayer has to be offered with a spirit of humility, with a profound self-awareness and self-deprecation, without any excuses and idealizations of our falls – of our incorrect behaviour. And that is one of our biggest tragedies: that is, when we constantly give excuses, not only inside us, but also outside us – to others, thus losing what little effort we had put into our personal daily struggle.

In short, we are saying that our prayer has to be like the proverbial tax collector's: *"**And the tax collector, standing afar, would not so much as raise his eyes to heaven, but beat his breast, saying, 'God, be merciful to me a sinner!**"* (Luke 18:13)

Even if we can't completely perceive our guilt, let us at least make some effort to, until such time as God opens the eyes of our soul.

Furthermore, there must be no enmity with any of our fellow men. This can be outlined in a multitude of ways, but let's mention two or three examples only.

It is expressed explicitly in the Lord's Prayer; that is: a necessary prerequisite for the Lord to forgive us, is if we forgive others –any others–

regardless of what they may have done to us. The reason for this is because we often hear: "Do you know, father, what so-and-so did to me, and yet you want me to forgive him, and to bid him 'good day'?"

Regardless of what others have done to us, we must forgive them. After all, during the Service prior to Holy Communion, what do we say, among other things? "...Firstly, reconcile yourself with those who sorrow you..." etc.

Of course that doesn't mean we are obliged to associate with everyone without exception; that would be impossible in practice; plus, it makes no sense and quite often it can also be harmful ... very harmful in fact. It is also not possible for all of us to be suited to everyone. It's a matter of idiosyncrasy; furthermore, many other factors are also involved. To use a colloquial term, "it's their right, and it's our right" (to become associated)... However, that which isn't our right –spiritually speaking– is to plot against others, to reproach and scorn those we don't feel suited to, or don't feel comfortable with. In other words (given that we are constantly questioned on this point): we must be on good terms with those we feel suited to, but even so, there shouldn't be too much outspokenness and familiarity with them, because that can eventually create many ugly side-effects: spiritual ones, but also social, psychological, and –why not– organic ones.

Therefore, we should be on good terms with those we feel suited to, but we should also be on good terms with those that we don't feel suited to, except we should remain detached from them – that is, from a relatively safe distance, so that we won't have too many "derailments" - be they by a neighbor or a relative or a colleague at work, or... or... or...

Elder Paisios used to say on this point "When you want to join two pieces of wood and those pieces aren't harmoniously matched through proper planing, no matter how hard you try to join them together with a screw and a bolt and keep tightening the screw, then, because they haven't been planed properly to fit harmoniously together, and the more you tighten them and not allow them to fit loosely, the more they will buckle and kick back. However, if they fit well together and have been harmonized by planing, then, with just a tiny quantity of glue they will stick together beautifully." You can understand what the blessed Elder Paisios meant here, as he would always find very suitable examples with which he could benefit any pilgrim whatsoever, and make him understand the spiritual inference that he wanted to convey, more clearly and more dynamically.

Prayer should also be accompanied by secret acts of charity – like those by Cornelius, whom God had hearkened to. The Lord is generally more pleased when He sees our secret spiritual struggle and our secret acts of charity. What are we told? "***The Lord, Who sees that which is in secret...***" We must give charities, but without advertising the act by claiming that we are supposedly benefiting others, or... or.... We resort to all sorts of excuses and we don't apply the Gospel's words: "***...when you do a charitable deed, do not let your left hand know what your right hand is doing.***" (Matthew 6:3). Thus, when the Lord sees our secret labours and our secret charities, and when He deems it appropriate, He will repay visibly – if that is deemed necessary... and if it is deemed useful. Thereafter, it's up to God... We shouldn't strive at all; no matter how hard we hide what we do –which is what we should do– then, at the moment God decides it is beneficial, He has ways of informing the others of our (secret) acts.

But even in general, we are not merely obliged to give charities in secret; we must be charitable at heart. "...with a heart that is ablaze", as Saint Isaac the Syrian says, "for all of Creation, even for serpents, for a-logical animals..." Pay attention to this awesome statement: The charitable heart cannot bear to see any harm being done to Creation. Even the slightest harm causes pain and arouses prayer in the charitable heart.

Also, a necessary prerequisite for prayer is the humbling of the body with fasting, prostrations, various kinds of ascesis, both in quantity and in quality. And let's not forget that, albeit the time for fasting is predetermined by our holy Church, nevertheless the time for continence is always a must, depending of course on the circumstance. For example, even after the Lenten fast is over, it is preferable on the Easter feast-day to have some restraint on the food we eat, rather than gorge ourselves freely. Restraint is also advised, for the eves of fasting periods, when we tend to eat extra quantities in order to "tolerate" the fasting restrictions of the three pursuant days. It is far more preferable to have a steadier schedule. But that is another matter. At any rate, there must be ascesis. And Orthodoxy is definitely ascetic.

Also, a correct prayer must project requests that are chiefly of spiritual dimensions, as the Lord Himself had said: "***But seek first the kingdom of God and His righteousness, and all these things shall be added to you.***" (Matthew 6:33) All other things will be given to you. In other words, we mustn't act "cheaply". Unfortunately, we hear certain things and we are sorrowed by them. Some say: "Pray, father, for my child, because he is giving exams, or, for his health etc..." Yes, all these things are a part of our lives. Parents' and children's worries are important... yes, yes, yes... BUT, we mustn't remain there. When we persevere that way, we behave in a "cheap" manner and merely display our spiritual shallowness.

And this kind of mentality sorrows us, both for those people's agonies, but also because they haven't got the proper spiritual stance. If they had the proper spiritual stance, they would have had less agony, and would have been more successful in their daily activities and –more importantly– they would have attained a much greater personal spiritual progress.

We must also pray with faith; not "simply believe" that God exists (which is a given fact, otherwise it would be senseless to pray – why pray to someone, if we don't believe He exists?) However, we need to completely trust God's Providence – that God will not let us be tested beyond our tolerance levels, and that He will give us a favourable outcome at the appropriate moment, provided it will be beneficial, for our eternal benefit and not only to our personal and temporary benefit, because quite often, these two will unfortunately inevitably contravene each other.

An Orthodox mien is also required in prayer. It's what the Lord had said: ***"God is Spirit, and those who worship Him must worship in spirit and truth."*** (John 4:24) It is unthinkable to be a heretic. All worship coming from heretics is hubris against God. Of course there are many other factors for the best possible fruition of our prayer. Among them are our tears, and our perseverance – that is, to remain steadfast in our prayers, and not pray only when we are in the mood for praying, which is a gross delusion. All the important ascetics proved their mettle by persevering during periods of neglectfulness. Above and beyond all else - we must observe all the commandments.

Praying is not an end in itself; it is a means for approaching closer to God. Our prime goal should be the discarding, the altering and the about-face of the old self, and not praying while clinging to our old habits, our passions and our weaknesses. That is also a huge delusion. In fact, when we insist on holding on to our passions -and fully aware that we are doing it - then quite often we will not be led to correct paths with those prayers. And, if you want to persevere in such prayers while clinging to those weaknesses and passions (which often do exist, unfortunately), and if we aren't careful, we can even fall into delusion. The first fruit of prayer is to become illumined so that we can discard those weaknesses of ours.

So, given those prerequisites, let's now examine and let's scrutinize the Jesus Prayer (the "Lord Jesus Christ, have mercy on me"), because, as we said, it is the most drastic and simultaneously the most effective method against our three greatest enemies.

Firstly, our first and foremost enemy is our very own self. With its habits, its weaknesses and its passions, which we more often than not do not even recognize, but instead, tend to regard them as virtues. What can we begin to mention? For example, when we say things like "I gave her a lesson", or "I gave her a piece of my mind", or "I took them down a peg or two", or "I settled them, once and for all"... and many such actions and dramatic situations. Our tragedy and the greatest injustice that we perpetrate against ourselves is that unfortunately, we don't realize, nor do we make any attempt to realize, our guilt opposite God…

Now, our second enemy is the devil, who, like a roaring lion roams about seeking to devour someone; like a roaring lion in the spiritual sense, which persistently seeks the prey that it will devour. Satan's psychology as we have mentioned before resembles more or less the psychology of a bad student, who remained in the same grade, not out of a weakness or any other logical explanation, but out of pure stubbornness, indifference and negligence. So, instead of seeking to improve his situation, that is, to focus on studying and passing his grade worthily, the bad student (the devil, in this example) paradoxically struggles, agonizes, hopes and seeks consolation in his attempts to seduce all his other co-students if possible, so that they too might remain in the same grade with him.

Well, Satan's psychology is somewhat similar… although, deep down, his psychology and his minions' is incomprehensible, because with what he does, over and over again, he only worsens his own situation in view of the coming terrible tribunal of the Supreme Judge on Judgment Day…

And our third serious enemy is the world, which, according to the Bible, resides within evil, with all its daily, anti-God displays in general. And, as the years go by, up until the days of the antichrist, the world will be going from bad to worse. Wherever one may look, there is sin, there is evil. Even if one looks up at the sky –as a certain soul once said to us: "it's quite possible that nothing good can be seen there either". Because –as he said- once, when he looked up towards the sky, he beheld an indecent banner trailing behind an airplane that was flying low and advertising something. It was an indecent image, which was actually visible to the naked eye from the earth below. In other words, sin prevails everywhere.

One might then ask: what should we do? Should we have phobias – when looking either up or down? Even if we are "up high", we are never safe for sure. No. We must have a system – an internal one we might say, an automatic spiritual mechanism – which can reject whatever is trash, whatever is not good, so that we don't accept it inside us… so that it doesn't become imprinted in our mind, because (let's not fool ourselves) it's not our eye's fault nor our vision's, but rather it's "the mind that sees and the mind that hears". In other words, whatever prods the mind and focuses our attention, signifies that there exists an inner motive of ours, and in this case, there is an underlying passion of ours, which focuses on certain images. If that passion didn't exist, we would be able to notice - without "looking". As Fr. Paisios also used to say to us, "we must observe absentmindedly, without being absentminded". That is, those sinful images shouldn't imprint themselves inside our being; because if we acquire a phobia in this regard, we suffer greater damage by the enemy.

In the first segment of the Jesus Prayer, we admit the divinity of Christ, Who suffered for us and instead of us – that is, in our stead and for our sake – thus fulfilling the relative prophecy of the scapegoat in the Old Testament.

In Christ is the fullness of godhood and humanity; because, if Christ wasn't God, then not only would He NOT be able to save us, but would Himself be in need of personal salvation. Christ, therefore, IS God. He is the Second Person of the Holy Trinity, Who willed to even take on human form. Of course this Incarnation was realized with the simultaneous will of the Father; that is, the Father condescended, and the Son-Logos became flesh – with the synergy of course of the Third Person of the Holy Trinity: the Holy Spirit.

We need to be fully aware that there is a difference, between the Time-less and eternal relations between the Three Persons of the Holy Trinity (the inter-family ones), and the individual salvific roles of the Three Persons of the Holy Trinity for the salvation of the entire world. In other words, the role that each Person of the Holy Trinity individually played for our salvation – both for us humans, as well for the angels and Creation.

However, as you yourselves can understand, all these points require specialized homilies;

therefore at this point we won't persist, so that we don't deviate from our main topic. The only thing that we are pointing out here is that we unfortunately underestimate and ignore the roles of the other Two Persons – of the Father and the Holy Spirit.

Now, as for the second segment of the Jesus Prayer, "have mercy on me, the sinner", we are admitting our guilt, even though we aren't aware of it. And it is imperative that we do so. Thus, having admitted our guilt, we invoke divine mercy. "Have mercy" means "have pity on me, Lord", which in turn is interpreted in various ways – such as "illumine me, Lord", as Saint Gregory Palamas used to say. He would constantly say "Lord, illuminate my darkness". As such, it can be interpreted as "illumine me, Lord", "fortify me, Lord", "heal me, Lord", and before all else, "forgive me, Lord" - at every moment, circumstance and temptation - but not the way that I, the impassioned and finite man want and judge. We repeat: no, not the way we want to judge, but the way God's infallible judgment would judge – that is, whatever is for our spiritual and eternal benefit. Why? Well, let's not hide behind our finger – we only care about having a good time, especially in this lifetime. God however, like the kind and wise father that He is, doesn't care about this transient lifetime. What does He care about? Well, our (hopefully eternal), personal and best possible spiritual restoration.

Quite often, we encounter a certain personal, professional or family misfortune… or, even worse, an illness, the death of a loved one. As much as all these may undoubtedly be very painful – no-one will say anything to the contrary – if we utilize them spiritually, they are a very significant, soul-saving, personal factor.

It is of course quite a different thing, when - very often - certain personal reckless actions with painful outcomes, both material and spiritual, are ascribed to God and not to ourselves, albeit of our own, morbid, pseudo-piety and a camouflaged disposition for self-vindication, whether we realize it or not. We commit blunders with the tendency to say: "Oh well… that was -after all- how the Holy Mother wanted it to be", when in fact we were responsible for not paying attention to our health, our finances, and a whole lot of other things.

Please pay close attention to this point; although, it cannot be analyzed in depth at present.

By repeating the Jesus Prayer, we truly live the blessed state of humility; where humility is not merely a group of fine words, nor is it about sitting rigidly in a pietistic manner, like pillars or statues – unnaturally – but, according to Saint Maximos, humility is the most realistic of states, consisting of a dual knowledge and awareness. First of all it consists of the awareness of God's power and glory and simultaneously an awareness of our own personal spiritual weakness.

However, for us to become familiarized with these two very vivid realities and states, we must make an effort. Otherwise, as intelligent or educated as we might be, we won't comprehend anything of these two aspects.

For example, how can we possibly comprehend or empirically experience the glory of God, if God Himself doesn't reveal a little of His immeasurable glory to us? Furthermore, all the Saints had become acquainted through personal experience with the power, the rage and the mania of Satan and the demons, as well as with human weakness and frailty and inadequateness, but simultaneously with God's salvific intervention, which in most cases was accompanied by a certain "theopty", a "theophany" (sighting of God), or at any rate with some kind of direct or indirect divine intervention. We often remark how God arranged matters and saved us from something which was certainly not a chance occurrence.

As for this Prayer: Not only in our wicked age, but also in the past, there have been some – even very pious – people, who maintained and still maintain that the Jesus Prayer is not destined for the laity, but only for monastics – even as far back as the time of Saint Gregory Palamas, who was one of the most fervent supporters of the Jesus Prayer. Of course what "Saint Gregory Palamas" is all about (whom we are unfortunately ignorant of), is not a subject that can be taken up at present. We need only mention that our Church has dedicated the Second Sunday of the Lenten Fast to him, because She regards his teaching as the model of genuine Orthodox spirituality. Thus, while on the first Sunday of Fasting we celebrate the victory of the Orthodox conscience - the victory of the Orthodox Faith - on the Second Sunday of the Lenten fast, the proper Orthodox spirituality is projected, through Saint Gregory Palamas – that is, the correct Orthodox spirituality – which must of course be the outcome of a correct Orthodox faith.

Thus, during the time of Saint Gregory Palamas, when a certain (otherwise pious) monk named Job heard Saint Gregory so insistently proposing this Jesus Prayer to everyone without exception – both the laity and monastics – he had objected. Suffice it to imagine that for a very long period of time – when Saint Gregory was at the Skete at Veria, but also when he was at the Sacred Retreat of Saint Savvas on the Holy Mountain and despite his innumerable duties, which he had delegated to other, competent persons – he would spend the rest of the week from Monday to Friday dedicated exclusively to the noetic Jesus Prayer. He officiated in church, received Holy Communion and settled all his other affairs, only on Saturdays and Sundays.

Thus, when the otherwise virtuous monk, Job, heard Saint Gregory Palamas suggesting the reciting of the Jesus Prayer by the laity also, he reacted and objected to Saint Gregory's suggestion. However, being a man of great virtue himself, he was in fact visited by an angel of the Lord, who instructed him to obey the opinion and heed the stance of Saint Gregory Palamas on the Jesus Prayer. That detail alone, which is just a minor one, proves just how God-sent this Prayer is.

But what am I saying? Even the Apostle Paul in his Epistle to Thessalonians had said the familiar quote "***pray without ceasing***" (1 Thess.5:17). Or elsewhere, where he had said "***I sleep, but my heart is vigilant***" (Song of Songs 5:2): while he was asleep, his heart remained alert, praying. What do we surmise from those words? That we must pray incessantly and that it is a feasible thing, and also, that what the Apostle said about the prayer is not an exaggeration or a figure of speech, but rather, those words –albeit incomprehensible- are in fact enormous spiritual realities, which are feasible for man - with God's intervention, naturally - provided man does all he humanly can in every area, including this area.

Saint Gregory also mentions that praying is preferable to and more necessary than our breathing. We do not cease breathing for even one second; therefore, we should likewise not stop praying. And our entire life, all of our moves and all of our actions should be a prayer.

These, as we said earlier, are not just fancy words; they are instructions.

In the upcoming synaxes, we shall be firstly examining what the three main stages of the Prayer are: as beginners, we should recite it in a whispering voice, just enough for the ear to hear what the mouth is uttering – especially when we are alone and are not perceived by others. Gradually, we should repeat it mentally – to hold onto it with our mind – and finally, God willing, hold onto it with our heart – that is, with our spiritual heart, with our entire being.

Then, as we continue with our homilies dear brethren, we shall explain that the only way to accomplish the Church's instructions regarding prayer – such as the ***"pray without ceasing"*** and the ***"I sleep, but my heart is vigilant"*** is by means of the Jesus Prayer – the "Lord Jesus Christ, have mercy on me".

That was all we had to say for the time being today. We shall continue, as always, next Saturday.

5.
THE FIRST STAGE OF THE PRAYER - ANSWERS TO QUESTIONS

In our previous synaxis dear brethren, we had touched – entirely epigrammatically – on certain main prerequisites that our prayer must absolutely fulfill so that it may be truly God-pleasing.

They are the following: First of all, our prayer has to be like the tax-collector of the parable; there must not be any enmity towards our fellow-man; in parallel with our prayer, we must attend to spiritual and material charities and above all, we must have a charitable heart towards all of Creation. Thereafter, the other prerequisites that we mentioned are: fasting (in the stricter and the broader sense); Orthodox ascesis with discernment; asking for things with spiritual dimensions; faith in divine Providence; the proper faith; a courageous spirit, patience, and several other things.

We then made reference to the Jesus Prayer, and how it is the most potent method of prayer against our three greatest enemies: our self, the "world" and the devil.

We also said that the words "have mercy" mean "have pity on", but not according to our own judgment; rather, according to the infallible will of God, for the sake of our spiritual (eternal) and final benefit. And finally, we proved that this prayer is also equally suitable for the laity - that it is not strictly for monastics alone. These were of course mentioned briefly and we are just reminding you of them.

However, before proceeding further, we deem it expedient and necessary to reply to any queries that might be submitted.

****

Your first query was an oral one. Someone asked if the Prayer can "stand on its own" without an accompanying obedience. And we replied that it most assuredly and definitely cannot stand on its own. That will naturally depend on the kind of relationship he has with his spiritual father (if one is a monk), or, if he is a layperson, on whether he has a spiritual father etc... Of course one of the first fruits of this Prayer – is most assuredly the finding of an experienced, proper and discerning spiritual father. When he is found, he should show obedience to him with the appropriate disposition, because obedience must also be in accordance with the desire of our holy Church. In other words, it must be observed with the proper conscience in order for it to be God-pleasing and fruit-bearing. Given that praying is also one of the commandments (as we said), it must not be isolated; if it is isolated, in absentia of the other commandments, not only will it NOT bring forth spiritual fruits, but will quite often bring all sorts of side-effects – both spiritual as well as psychological ones. Therefore, in this sense, we outrightly declare that it is inconceivable for the Prayer to lack the spirit of obedience – that is, without any obedience to the commandments of our holy Church.

And in verification of the aforementioned dear brethren, let us read an excerpt from Abba Dorotheos, who makes reference to the construction and the assemblage of the soul's virtues.

Says Abba Dorotheos: "*...but how is the edifice of the soul constructed? We can be taught exactly how it is done, by observing the construction of a visible house; he who wants to build a material house must first secure it on all sides and raise the edifice at the same time, that is, all its four sides, and not attend to the one wall while neglecting the others, because that way, he gains nothing. He merely goes into futile and dangerous pains, plus a whole lot of expenses. Well, the same thing occurs with the soul. Man must absolutely not neglect any aspect of his spiritual edifice. He must raise it symmetrically.*"

That is exactly what Abba John Kolovos also implies when he says:

"I want man to attain a little of each virtue and not do what some others do, who struggle for only one virtue and persist in that one indiscriminately, laboring only for that one, while neglecting the other virtues. It could be that they may even have a certain preference for that one virtue, which is why

they aren't disturbed by the passion that is opposed to that virtue. Thus, they are fooled and burdened by the other passions and are suffocated by them and – unfortunately – are not in the least concerned about that; they are instead under the illusion – the impression – that they are supposedly making a huge spiritual achievement. They unfortunately resemble the one who builds a wall and raises it as much as he can, focusing all his attention, his labours, to the raising of that one wall, with the impression that he has achieved something grand, by gazing solely at the immense height of that wall. But he doesn't realize that if a strong wind were to come along – or an earthquake (even a mild earthquake) – it will bring down that wall, because – regrettably – that wall is standing all alone, without any connection and unity with other walls. And furthermore, he cannot even prepare a roof (for himself) upon a single wall, because he would remain exposed on all the other sides. Therefore that is not how it should be done; instead, he who wishes to build his house properly (his spiritual house) and make for himself a proper roof, must raise the edifice on all sides and secure it from every danger".

I believe, dear brethren, that all these points are very clear. So, after all that has been said, one can clearly see why the Prayer won't "stand on its own" without obedience; and not only without obedience, but also without the implementation of all the other virtues without exception. We mentioned these details, because a query was specifically submitted as to the "relationship between the Prayer and obedience". As such, yes, obedience is imperative.

As for the spirit of obedience – which of course is multifaceted, but now is not the time to expand on it – the only thing that we are epigrammatically highlighting is that obedience must be exercised, but only in a manner that will be acceptable to God. In other words our motives before God must be absolutely spiritual, absolutely pure; then, if and when God deems appropriate, He (being God) will find ways to improve us, and, both in the matter of obedience and in many other matters, will open new and better paths for us. Because, if the Jesus Prayer is isolated from obedience and all the other virtues, then it will be anything but a prayer, and instead of being a noetic prayer it will result in a whole lot of damages, a whole lot of spiritual perversions – depending of course on the case and the circumstances.

Certain other queries have also been expressed personally. First of all, they asked me about interpersonal relations with relatives. My instinctive thought suggested that they had asked me because, as mentioned in our previous gathering, there must be no enmity during the time of prayer. Most assuredly there should be no enmity.

However that doesn't mean it is compulsory to have relationships with everyone – be they a relative or a neighbor, or a colleague at work. In other words, we should have a closer, caring relationship with those that we are compatible with. But, with those who -for one reason or another- we aren't suitably matched, we should be caring towards them, but from an adequately safe distance, with a safety margin, so that we don't suffer various side-effects.

This of course is only a generalization, because many things are dependent on our final, personal relationships: the kind of affiliation, obligation, commitment or needs that our fellow-man has, the situation he is in, how we judge it, etc... These things of course cannot be placed in molds; it is a matter of discernment and obedience to a discerning spiritual guide or Elder. For example if we have a grandfather at home who is in effect a grumpy and demanding character, it doesn't mean we should bend to his every whim. That wouldn't be feasible. Because in the end, with all our personal fatigue – both physical and emotional – we will end up excessively tired, beyond our limits, we will lash out against him and blurt out everything "retroactively, and with compound interest", as the colloquial saying goes. It is a thousand times better to give less to grandfather, depending on our tolerance level, and chiefly, according to our judgment. I mean, it isn't a sin –technically, and not in essence- if we aren't 100% honest with him, without this implying that we must resort to lying. A lie never obtains blessings. It is preferable to discreetly ("here is wisdom") avoid upsetting him - avoid upsetting him in a

God-pleasing manner of course, and not in the manner that people in the world resort to – that is, by quarrelling and spouting "heavy" truths at him and in the long run infecting ourselves with bitterness, without sorting out the issue, and instead of arriving at a positive outcome, by actually causing him damage.

For example, we should have a different stance for our parents, another stance for someone else, another stance for those towards whom we have an obligation or a professional dependency. Like we said, it's a matter of discernment. At any rate, we aren't obligated to have relationships with everyone. In fact, quite often this also has no meaning, nor is it feasible; it is cheap, and more importantly, it's even detrimental.

These points of course are only generalizations.

Now, another related question that was posed with regard to human relations is the matter of whether we should break our fast for the sake of certain relatives or colleagues – for example when we need to go on a visit, or when we're invited somewhere, etc… Our reply – epigrammatically – is that Pharisaism was a fashion chiefly during Christ's time. Nowadays, it isn't exactly a fashion; we could say it's quite the opposite in most cases. Back then, when someone fasted, he would be praised by everyone. Now, if you fast, they make fun of you. So, the breaking of a fast is not so much about gluttony (although it can be of course), but is mainly about a confession of faith. "I fast, because the Church says so". That's why, in our humble opinion, we shouldn't break our fast, because if we do, it's like denying the very thing that we believe in. This - we think - is the main reason that we shouldn't break our fast. Let them say what they want, as long as we don't reciprocate with "spiritual retaliation fire", words and comments, or be critics and the suchlike. You understand what I mean…

And you should bear in mind that all these things have repercussions on prayer – that is, the one is not independent of the other. That's the reason we are responding to these questions, as independent as they may appear to be of prayer.

Another question now is whether it is permissible to be "chilly" during prayer – in the sense that "if we aren't in the mood, must we pray?" "Is prayer God-pleasing then?" We will of course also touch on this important topic, in our upcoming, humble, family gatherings. However, seeing as this question has been posed, we might mention in advance that it is a mistake to believe that we should pray only when we are in the mood for it, and with the corresponding spiritual disposition. Isn't that what our popular wisdom says: "With eating also comes the appetite"? This also applies to spiritual matters. Because quite often one may begin praying with zeal, then, for one reason or another, whether he is to blame or not, loses his initial zeal, his initial solemnity. But you should note that the opposite can also occur: One may commence praying under pressure, that is without zeal for one reason or another, then suddenly the "heavens may rain down" and he finds himself in a state that he could never have foreseen previously. But no matter what, that which is important and should preoccupy us, is not whether the heavens will or won't "rain down" Divine Grace, but rather if there is a proper disposition to persevere.

Heavenly "victory wreaths" are also woven depending on the sacrifice and the effort that we make – and always with discretion of course. But, as we have already mentioned, he who prays properly (and given that God is always a Father and desirous of giving us joys that are strictly for our benefit), will, sooner or later, experience moments of inexpressible joy. If you will, this can be seen as a consolation that God gives us during our spiritual struggle, in order to push us onward and instill added courage so that we can continue with that spiritual struggle of ours; but it can also assuredly be for many other reasons, such as incrementing our initial faith as well our knowledge of God, which is the most important thing.

And yet, in spite of our labours, it must be perceived as a product of God's Grace, because God is not bound by our toils and our disposition for perseverance. That's why the "Grace" of God is in fact a Gift of His. And woe betide the person who seeks charismas (gifts) from God in order to become boastful.

Now, as for another, related query:

It is preferable to say fewer prayers, content-wise, and not recite them hurriedly and anxiously (in the desire, that is, to experience them and understand them), rather than recite more prayers without the appropriate attention, having the recital of many prayers as an end in itself. We need to "assimilate" the words of a prayer, and not gulp down spiritual nourishment "unchewed", because that will generate side-effects and won't produce many spiritual fruits.

As Fr. Paisios used to say, we need to grasp the meaning of the words when saying the Prayer – to sense the Prayer - and not merely repeat it the way the "tick-tock" of a clock sounds (that is, mechanically); we need to live the Prayer and "digest" it thoroughly inside us, by being aware to Whom we are addressing it, and what we are beseeching Him for.

Now we shall respond to another pertinent question on the relations between the divine and the human element. We had mentioned that we often attribute our own foul play to a will of God (due to naiveté and spiritual immaturity - not to mention sometimes –unfortunately– on account of a camouflaged insolence). That is, we erroneously say "Oh well, if Christ wanted it, what can we do?" or, "If it was the will of God...", when it was anything BUT the will of God.

To this scalding question we would reply –entirely epigrammatically as always– that the divine element intervenes, only when the human factor has previously and wholly exhausted itself – with the appropriate prerequisites and the proper conscience of course. This is clearly apparent, both in the New Testament and throughout Patristic Literature. For example: Please take note of this. After resurrecting Jairos' daughter, Christ immediately instructed those present to give the girl some food to eat, which would help her regain her physical-mental powers. But –one might ask- couldn't the Lord have done things in such a way that (after being raised from the dead) the girl would also have her physical as well as her mental powers fully restored, at the same time as her resurrection from the dead? Of course He could have! But with this instruction, the Lord was also intentionally making a clear distinction between His divine act (which was the resurrecting) and the human act (which was the people's giving the girl some food to invigorate her).

Now, so that this stance by Christ won't be regarded as a chance incident, let's also mention the even more familiar case – of Lazarus, who was also raised from the dead. When Christ resurrected him four days after his death (with the familiar words "Lazarus, come outside!") what did our Lord say after that? He instructed the watchers-on to remove Lazarus' burial shroud, when that could have been done automatically by Him.

However this didn't only apply in the New Testament; we can also observe it in the Old Testament just as clearly, in many instances and contexts – that is, to which point God intervenes. Let's mention another example – one that pertains to the Israelites. While they were wandering in the Sinai desert for forty whole years, God kept sending them the manna from heaven; but, as soon as the Israelites stepped foot on the Promised Land, then the flow of manna from God ceased automatically. Why? Because the Israelites would thenceforth be responsible for cultivating the fertile land themselves, and producing whatever they needed for survival.

These points of course are just a first response to the subject of relations between the divine and the human factors. To discuss this on a more theoretical basis, we should take a look at what the Orthodox Church says. She says that collaboration between the human and the divine factors is imperative. Whatever belongs to the human predisposition (which must be expended) must necessarily be done by man. Therefore the notion of absolute predestination which had been introduced in the West by the blessed Augustine does not apply. Nor does the Muslim notion of "kismet" (destiny), or what we Orthodox (woefully) tend to mutter: "it was thus written..."

Of course a whole lot of other parameters apply in the divine factor, which cannot be expounded right now. As it is, they exceed every human intellect and power.

We tend to ask "Who can know the mind of the Lord?" Why is that? Well, my beloved brethren, it is because, just as God's essence cannot be understood, likewise, God's Will may be beneficial deep down, however the way He operates cannot be understood. The only sure thing that we know is that –finally- God will judge each person in a unique manner, but very justly.

We shall not expound this point further, because we will need a large number of homilies to exhaust the topic.

Some other questions that were posed were: "The Fathers lived in the desert and achieved the things that they achieved. How can we, who are laypeople in the world, manage?"

Well, first of all, we shouldn't go to extremes, such as "it's all or nothing". We can try to emulate the Saints' methods gradually. For instance: Did they live in the desert? Well, during a certain time of the day that suits us, in a certain corner of our home or somewhere else, we can create for ourselves our own little desert. Were they completely alienated from others? Well, we can likewise limit our own social communications, with fewer social contacts. Thus, if we are proper and objective and genuine, Christ will eventually inform the others, secretly, that we weren't doing it because we were avoiding them or because we supposedly didn't love them, but that we were doing it for a personal, spiritual reason. We can thus limit certain other, redundant (and even harmful we might say) displays of ours, in order to allow us to dedicate time for more spiritual exercises for ourselves; in this case, to dedicate more time to the Prayer. This will not be a cause for boredom and grief, but will in fact give us actual joy.

God has other demands and expectations from those who live outside the world, and other demands from us. God provides us also with opportunities for catharsis and sanctification, because the temptations and unforeseen happenings that each day has in store for us are so many, that if we were to apply the evangelical commands to all of them, they would be more than enough to ensure our sanctification and our spiritual progress.

Both unfortunately and fortunately, the insults, the ungratefulness, the scorn, the calumnies, the ugly images, the sights, are, from one aspect (which is why we said 'fortunately') in fact a marvelous opportunity for spiritual ascent and spiritual victory wreaths. But, we must be careful here: we should never strive for these to come; that is by no means proper. But let's not go into further detail right now...

What we are saying now, is that when these things come before us without our will, we should do what we must to oppose them. That way, we will be purged of those involuntary temptations and will progress spiritually. You can understand what we mean by this: we are, in other words, subject to spiritual examinations.

At this point, let's mention an event that the blessed Elder Paisios had narrated to us: When living ascetically at Konitsa for a time, he would pray to God most fervently to humble him. Well, the next time that the blessed Elder went to receive Holy Communion at the church in Konitsa per the customary rubric, the moment he (being a monk) entered the Inner Sanctum to participate in the Divine Liturgy like he always did, well, that one time, the same priest who officiated every other time told the Elder entirely unexpectedly, abruptly and suddenly and for no apparent reason, to leave the Sanctum immediately and to seat himself -imagine!- among the laity. Well, naturally, the Elder Paisios at first became humanly upset and astounded, but he immediately remembered how long he had been beseeching God to humble him; so he thought to himself: "Now that the opportunity has presented itself, should I let it go to waste?" So, after this occurrence, the blessed Elder glorified God for that spiritual opportunity which He had sent him.

I think, dear brethren, that this incident is an extremely indicative and a very beneficial one. No further comments are necessary.

And now, the reverse example; If you will, those who don't make any spirited effort to apply the commandments when they are in the world, then, usually, when God deigns and they remove themselves from the world but do not change their mindset and do not repent, they will likewise fail. But let's not persist further with details on this query.

Another query now, which was posed: "How is it possible, father, to not see evil everywhere, given that it exists?"

The answer is: by thinking positive thoughts. As man becomes cleansed, he will see everything around him much clearer, whereas another, reversely, will judge the things around him based on his own perception. So, as we said, we shouldn't be in fear of our sinful environment, but instead, just observe everything and everywhere "vacantly"; after all, "the mind observes and the mind hears". If we cleanse our mind then every impure thing will not penetrate us. How can we clarify this? Well, there will be an automatic, spiritual defence mechanism inside us, which will not allow anything non-beneficial to penetrate our deeper being. Or, to limit our analysis, there will be a personal, internal spiritual "bio-cleansing", whereby anything unsuitable that penetrates us will be automatically cleansed on its own. But that is another state altogether, so let's not analyze it any deeper for the time being.

Beneficial to all the aforementioned are positive thoughts, as we pointed out. Again, as we were told by the blessed Elder Paisios, man initially struggles against evil thoughts by shunning them and bringing positive thoughts to mind. Eventually, a soul-saving internal vacating will ensue, whereby man will have no thoughts whatsoever – positive or evil ones.

And this –please take note– is what the Elder also told us: that this vacating is by far superior to positive thoughts. Of course this truly blessed state has no relation to the stupefaction – or, better still – the numbing that is caused by the various psychopharmaceuticals, with their numerous other side-effects and dependencies.

And one last theological query that was posed: "How did the devil become acquainted with evil?"

Saint John the Damascene replies to this, saying that Satan hadn't been given a single trace of evil by God. But, by not having accepted the illumination and the honour that the Creator had given him, then, through his own (albeit God-given) free will, he was transformed from his original, natural state to a contrary state, and exalted himself before God Who had created him.

So you see, the devil's central aberration was pride, in that he sought to revolt against God. And, given that he first had chosen to distance himself from what was good, he automatically ended up in evil; because evil is nothing more than the absence of good. That is to say, evil does not exist by nature. This is a recognized Patristic position.... Just like the dark: What is darkness? Darkness does not actually consist of something… it is simply the deprivation of light. Thus, just as the good is a spiritual light, likewise evil is a spiritual darkness.

To summarize, therefore, and to speak a little more theologically, evil doesn't have a hypostasis of its own. It is nothing more than the absence of good. That's how Satan with his pride deprived himself of the good that he had by nature – the result of that deprivation being his downfall into evil. And he not only fell into it, but even persisted in it thereafter. That was how the saying "To not fall is of the angels" was coined. Of course this motto applies after the advent of Christ, because before Christ, the angels could fall. But let's not digress… So, "To not fall is angelic; to fall is human", but "to fall and persist is demonic". In other words, it is an angelic trait when one doesn't fall. To fall is human, provided we get up again as quickly as possible. But to persevere in the fall is by far a demonic thing.

And to make this point even more vivid, let's again mention an example from your familiar Elder Paisios:

Once, as he was praying for all of Creation with such pain and love, he even prayed for the demons. He felt such pain, even for those very demons, that he would even say "My God, have mercy on them, for they too are Your creatures – regardless if they ended up where they did". And as the blessed Elder himself said, a demon appeared before him in the form of a large dog that mocked him and laughed sarcastically, demonically, poking his tongue far out, as if saying to him "No matter what you do, this is the way we like to be".

So, dear brethren, that's what we had to say for today (entirely epigrammatically of course) with regard to the queries – which were very many. Albeit having used up most of the time of our regular synaxis here, nevertheless we regarded them significant enough to be answered.

At any rate, I think that all these things are indissolubly linked with prayer – that is, for the purpose of maximizing the fruits of the Jesus Prayer.

Now, at this point, we can say straight away that, for the first phase of the Jesus Prayer ("Lord Jesus Christ, have mercy on me"), it is recommended - for those of us who are spiritual novices - to practice saying the Prayer in a whisper. By "whisper" we mean just enough for the ear to hear what the mouth is saying. This of course is appropriate for when we are entirely alone and can't be perceived by others. Therefore, if we are entirely alone, we can even recite the prayer out loud if we want to.

But we mustn't forget something: That God is pleased by - and delights in - our privately accomplished, personal spiritual labours, and not in advertising. Quite often, perhaps out of a good intention, out of love and sorrow, we imagine (although we are robbed somewhat by the little urchin here) that we should announce the good that we do for another's benefit. But see how the word of God throughout time comes and tells us the opposite (which, we believe, is familiar). What does the word of God say? ***"Don't let your left hand know what your right hand is doing"*** (Matt.6:3). And yet, we forget that God can secretly inform the others' hearts, without any personal harm to us. Thus, when we're alone, we can recite the prayer in a whisper; but when we're in a public place and unfortunately haven't yet become accustomed to saying the Prayer mentally, what do we do? Then, we can say the Prayer in a whisper, but not in an externally obvious way. And how is that done? Well, we simply move our tongue behind closed lips – so that it touches against our teeth and palate, inside our mouth. If again for some reason we cannot recite the Prayer (but now is not the time to discuss it, because the reasons can be many) then it is preferable, rather than remaining inactive, to recite a segment of the Prayer, or even one word from it... for example "My Jesus… my Jesus… My Jesus…" or "have mercy… have mercy… have mercy…". The mention alone of Jesus' name can generate an immense internal spiritual bliss and personal spiritual fruition.

We must therefore say the Prayer in a whisper to begin with, when we are basically undistracted, but also when we are preoccupied with other activities. So, we stress it once again

– because we are constantly asked about it: We must recite the Prayer, both when we are not distracted by anything and also during our other activities. In other words, there is no unsuitable moment for reciting the Prayer. And we need to find time; we have no excuse for pretending that we can't find any time during the day when we are undistracted. As much as we may think that there is no such available time, there is no excuse. Because, if we were to monitor ourselves as to where and how we consume our time during the day, we will all discover that we spend our time on things which may perhaps not be harmful per se, but are surely futile, to say the least. Only then will we become aware that we can always find some spare time; and the time that we can dedicate to prayer is not only time not wasted – not even to the detriment of the everyday essentials of living – instead, it even creates a state of solemnity and alertness, which make us more efficient in our daily chores, and – by repeating the Prayer - also avoid many traps, many unforeseen things which, if not handled properly with spiritual alertness and the illumination through the Prayer, we will be wasting far more time tackling them in a different way; but not only that; we will even be harmed spiritually and be exposed to a variety of other damages.

Thus, as already mentioned – and in parallel with all kinds of activities – it is not simply permitted, but is in fact imperative to repeat the

Prayer. Even while a housewife is cooking, or ironing; or when someone is travelling or waiting in a queue for an official document and is anxious and somewhat annoyed because it's taking too long, well, he can utilize that time wonderfully, by repeating the Prayer. Even if we are working in our field or our office or while undertaking a responsible chore, we can pause every now and then, and connect with the "Centre". What is the "Centre"? It is God Himself.

Even when we go to sleep, or wash ourselves, or are already in bed, it is no shame... we should say the Prayer, everywhere and at any time. Because quite often, the enemy attacks us even more fiercely when in bed and during our sleep.

There is no shame in mentioning these things. In a nutshell, we are saying that there is no unsuitable moment wherein we can't say the Prayer, because the devil is always on the alert to attack us, therefore we must fight back, even if laying in bed, but not only when laying down. The same applies with studying. We are constantly asked: "Can we read the New Testament in bed?" "Yes, in bed also, but not only in bed."

In closing, let's mention something from the "Ladder" by Saint John of Sinai, in order to be more convincing in what we've said. A certain renowned ascetic was forced to go to an unclean place in order to drive out unclean thoughts, because he was unable to pray the way he wanted, during a certain synaxis. So he went to that unclean place in order to drive away those unclean thoughts, which the wily demons wanted to implant in his mind, because he had no other choice...

These, my beloved brethren, are what we had to offer to your love today, on the subject of the Prayer.

God willing, we shall continue next Saturday, at the same time of course.

6.
THE METHOD AND THE STAGES OF THE PRAYER
(...pursuant to questions and answers)

Let's slowly get into today's topic. But before commencing, my beloved in-Christ brethren, let's respond to three or four queries that have been posed.

The first query, which was public, had to do with the development of the Jesus Prayer over time; that is, how it developed during the passage of ecclesiastic history.

And we had replied that there are mentions, in many places of the New Testament. For example, in the gospel of the Ten Lepers, we read of the specific plea by the lepers: "***Jesus, Master, have mercy on us***" (Luke 17:13). Or, in the excerpt of the born blind man: what did that man persistently say? "***Jesus, Son of David, have mercy on me!***" (Luke 14:35). And of course there are similar invocations in various other places in the Gospel.

All those invocations are purely the incessant prayer of the Church, which we hear whenever the laity responds to each petition by the Priest with the words "Lord have mercy". Well, the Jesus Prayer is simply an extended and more complete rendition of that petition.

The Jesus Prayer was familiar from the time of Abba Macarius, as mentioned in the Gerontikon (Book of Elders), during the years 300-390 A.D., where it says: "***There were some who asked the Abba Macarius, saying: "How should we pray?" And the Elder said to them: "There is no need for verbosity, only extending one's arms and saying "Lord, as You desire and as You know, have mercy". If spiritual war is imminent, "Lord help me"; and He knows what is beneficial and will be merciful to us.***"

Loosely translated, these words say: "Certain people asked the Abba Macarius –who was greatly famous as an insightful ascetic- and said to him "How should we pray, Elder?" And the Elder replied: "It is not necessary to say many things; just to raise our arms (and our souls of course) and only say "Lord, show me Your mercy, the way that You know and the way You want". Should there be an ongoing battle, a certain temptation, we should say "Lord, help me". And God knows what is for our benefit, so He will give the most suitable outcome, at the most suitable moment, and will be merciful to us."

However, Saint John –the author of the Ladder- (around 570-640 A.D.) mentions the following: "Let the remembrance of Jesus be joined to your breath and then you shall learn the benefit of quietude". That is, the remembrance of Christ should be joined to your breath and be continuous, and then you will become acquainted with the benefit that comes from godly quietude.

Elsewhere, the same, God-sighting author of the Ladder says very vividly: "By the name of Jesus, thrash all opposers, for there is no mightier weapon in heaven and on earth." In other words, attack your enemies with Christ's name, which are: yourself, the demons and the world. There is no other, more powerful or drastic weapon, either in heaven or on earth, than Christ's Name – than the Prayer in Christ's Name.

Now, with the opportunity of this truly lovely question, let's mention that it wasn't only the matter of the Jesus Prayer, but also many other things which had evolved and developed within the Church, in the Holy Spirit, such as the feast days, Worship, Hymnography, and a whole lot of other things that pertain to Orthodox spirituality… art, etc..

Let's mention a striking example: How do you imagine that the Divine Liturgies were performed during the first years? It may seem strange now, to us, but at the time, each priest –as expected, and depending on his theological education and his personal preparation - would offer certain improvised prayers, of course based on the general model of the Last Supper. And that was how the Precious Gifts were transformed into Body and Blood of Christ. That's how it had begun. And where did we end up today? For obvious reasons, we ended up avoiding dogmatic mistakes, so that we might have a better and richer worship etc… from the Divine Liturgies of the Apostolic Commands, of Saint Mark, of Saint James the Brother of Christ, of Saint Gregory the Theologian, of Saint Basil the Great, and the one most familiar to us – the Divine Liturgy of Saint John the Chrysostom – all of them so wonderfully rich. So, you now have an idea how things evolved for the Divine Liturgy. Anyway, these were just a few words on the evolution of the Prayer and the Divine Liturgy.

What I do want, however, with the opportunity of this wonderful query, is for you to hold on to the following detail:

Whatever our Church has in use, has been "polished" to perfection. Which is why we shouldn't be so concerned about how it evolved to this day, as the benefit of this detail is minimal. Instead, above and beyond everything, let's preoccupy ourselves on how to better utilize it more correctly, in a more God-pleasing manner for our personal spiritual benefit, and how we should respect it in the appropriate manner.

Now, another query is: "What is blasphemy against the Holy Spirit?" Given that it is indeed unforgiveable -according to the Gospel- there are those who are afraid that they may have actually committed it and will never be forgiven. Well, although the proper interpretations are many, basically blasphemy against the Holy Spirit is when one ascribes God's energies to the devil, and especially when it is done out of a malevolent intention. An example is when the Pharisees said of Christ that He drives out demons with the power of Satan! (Matthew 12:24)

But, to avoid expanding too much on this topic, we will say the following: that complete impenitence is an offence against the Holy Spirit and that by definition this impenitence is, understandably, unforgiveable. In practical terms, finally, what is blasphemy against the Holy Spirit? It is the persistence in not repenting. For this reason, we who struggle should not have any fear; there is no unforgivable sin for anyone who struggles – provided he repents of course. And, we shall not be condemned because we have sinned, but will be condemned if we don't repent for those things that we committed and sinned.

Also, one other query refers to the discernment of thoughts – if they originate from the enemy or not - in other words, how we can discern this. My dear brethren, for us it is not simply safer; it is totally necessary to ask a discerning Elder. Otherwise we will surely suffer damage sooner or later. Whereas if we consult a discerning Elder, he will give us the appropriate answer. However, even beyond this, with the predisposition for humility that we have for externalizing and depositing our thoughts to someone else, well, this stance alone moves God – of course provided this predisposition of ours is a totally honest one. Seeing this predisposition of ours, God will enlighten us and lead us onto a proper spiritual path.

This has been the experience of the Fathers, and this has been the order of our Church and Her tradition: the exposition of our thoughts and our sins.

And now, one last question – perhaps a more difficult one.

This question is about whether the conscience that we have is a cultural product – whether it has been imposed on us externally, by others.

Undoubtedly, conscience has been implanted in man by God. Conscience per se is not the result of the various cultures and legislations. Of course depending on the innumerable factors (which cannot be detailed now, due to time limitation), conscience can be shaped, refined, blunted, impassioned etc...

At this point we can say that – before the Fall of Adam – there was only one pertinent space in man's soul, and it was none other than a "moral conscience"; that is, the conscience that rendered Adam aware of what he was doing. Because, if Adam didn't have a moral conscience, he wouldn't have been able to perceive his sin, and as such, wouldn't have been responsible for it. Thus, instead of repenting after having sinned before God, Adam said: "My God, it wasn't my fault; it was the woman that **<u>You</u>** gave me". Notice how all the blame falls mainly on the "You" – in other words, he more or less said "You are to blame, God!"

But with this excuse of his, Adam had fatally transposed guilt from the space of his conscience to another space which hadn't existed before. And that space is what we refer to nowadays as "subconscious". It was at that moment, when, for the first time in human history the subconscious was created and was to be thereafter inherited by the entire human race and – as analytically mentioned in other homilies – was to be mankind's tragic element, both in times of peace and of war. No matter how saintly a person is, no-one is without a subconscious. Only Jesus Christ – the incarnate Logos of the Father, Who descended from heaven – didn't have a subconscious. Of course in the case of the Saints, it is through their constant personal struggle that they have succeeded in gradually eradicating what we call the "subconscious".

But nowadays, this displacement, this driving out of guilt is being done increasingly systematically. Why? Because modern man is not only annoyed by any reference to sins, but even by simply hearing the sound of the word "sin". He is unimaginably annoyed by it. So, what does he want? He wants – if possible - to abolish the word "sin", even from the dictionary. And the poor suffering wretch – modern-day man – is convinced that by not wanting to face his sin, he is supposedly liberated from his personal, unrestrained sin. In other words, the epitome of self-delusion! The reason is that sin cannot be expunged; man simply doesn't see it, even though it exists. And given that it exists, it gnaws away at modern man, unfortunately from head to toe, at his entire being, and it disintegrates his soul and his body – and much worse than that: it disintegrates him spiritually, throughout time, eternally.

So much – for the time being – with regard to your truly interesting queries.

Now let's move on, to the subject of the Jesus Prayer.

As mentioned earlier on, it is better to say the Prayer in a whisper. For all of us who are undoubtedly beginners, it requires strict perseverance and steadfast struggle – painful, tough, ruthless struggle. The whole struggle mainly lies in focusing our nous (mind) on the meanings of the words that we utter. In other words, we need to pay attention and mean what we are saying. We need to let the words sink well into us: "Lord Jesus Christ, have mercy on me". We need to understand the meanings of those words. We need to be sated by those words. Subsequently, at that moment, the most beneficial thing is to pay attention to what we are uttering.

Of course unruliness is a characteristic of the mind – to wander off here and there. As the Fathers used to say, our mind is like a young tramp that likes to wander about, here and there. That's how our mind likes wandering off to various matters here and there. But, wherever God intervenes, everything is stabilized. This is what happens in the case of our mind, when God intervenes: we will have an undisturbed

Prayer, that is, one without any interruptions, without our thinking of other matters.

But for God to intervene, what must necessarily precede it on our part – exhaustively, one could say – is human effort, sincere human willingness.

And when we say something should be "correct", we mean it should always be with prudence.

What we would like to stress at this point, is that during the time of prayer, we must not adopt any thought whatsoever. Not only harmful thoughts, not only the useless ones, but even the most "beneficial" ones. The word "beneficial" is in quotation marks because in the long run, during the time of prayer they are anything but beneficial. It is only a sly trap by the devil, because what is most beneficial during the Prayer is to pay attention –without imaginings– to the words of the Prayer. We should say it in simpler words to make it clearer: we shouldn't focus our mind anywhere – not on churches, not on monasteries, not on pilgrimages, not on elders or the words of elders, not on radiant faces, nor on saints or icons, nor on the various conversations that we've had with enlightened people and had become enchanted and had been helped by them...

None of these things is necessary and beneficial or gives us strength and enlightens us in our personal struggles, provided we think about them at other times and moments. However, to put all of them aside is extremely painful at first, because we and our mind have both been overindulgent. So, although it is a painful thing, nevertheless it is always a beneficial and necessary one.

Says the blessed Hagiorite, Elder Joseph of Vatopedion, in one of his letters where he gives his advice regarding the Prayer: *"Only be careful, when saying the Prayer, to not concede to imaginings, because the divine is kind-less – that is, it doesn't have any kind, it cannot be imagined, it cannot be coloured, it is beyond perfect, it cannot comply with human contemplations; it acts like a subtle breath within our intellects."* It acts like a subtle breath –not because it actually IS a subtle breath, but because the divine cannot be described. But let's not fool ourselves; it is, after all, obvious that a lot of effort is required, not just one day's worth (we unfortunately seek to achieve the Prayer in one evening). A lifetime of effort is required. Because especially during the time of prayer, the devil fights us with a particular vengeance, method and mania: we are attacked with lewd, horrific and bizarre thoughts of all kinds and from all directions; we are attacked by negligence; very many suppressed and forgotten things rise to the surface; we are confronted by an untimely anger – which sometimes is a very intense one – both during prayer and after it. Various pending chores and obligations come to mind (don't forget this... don't forget the other... this is necessary... that is necessary… etc). All of these things are exaggerated by the cunning one, as well as by our own inexperience. He exaggerates them to an extreme degree, so that although (while in prayer) we tell ourselves to not forget this or that etc., when we finish praying, we remember nothing of all the things that had overwhelmed us and on account of our inexperience, had considered it absolutely necessary to tackle them.

Thus, the cunning one overwhelms us with all sorts of supposedly compulsory cares and in one word, pummels us from every possible direction, ruthlessly, by naturally exploiting our own inexperience. This is why – among other things – it is more beneficial to repeat the Prayer in a whisper, so that even if the mind wanders, at least the uttered words remain and their benefit over time is not at all insignificant.

Besides, when the ear can hear what the mouth utters, the mind can more easily return to itself from its wandering and its distraction, and continue with its task of praying. Otherwise, when a spiritual novice does not whisper the Prayer, the mind wanders off and who knows after how long God will illumine him and he will eventually understand that he needs to resume the Prayer that he had begun to recite.

Of course we need to clarify at this point that thoughts per se are never a sin, when we don't accept them, when we don't "disturb" them, when we don't add "fertilizer" to them. You understand what this means. Then, out of sorrow for the assault by those thoughts on us, not only are we not harmed, we are actually promoted spiritually – that is, we are rendered wiser in our struggle against passions. There are, therefore, temptations that can promote us spiritually; and, the more that one struggles, the more powerful his enemies become, when they spring up on the spiritual front. This is a spiritual law.

And the enemy implements this intervention with thoughts, in order to make us despair and completely abandon the Prayer –not only because we supposedly don't benefit by it, but also because we sin even more during praying, inasmuch as we are preoccupied with thoughts that are so ugly, so weird, so unacceptable, that we hadn't even considered them before beginning to pray.

Unfortunately, here also is a bitter truth: that we all gradually fall into this trap of the devil and we either become disillusioned, or abandon the prayer, or drift into melancholy - or in the least - we begin to converse with our thoughts and thus lose the content of the Prayer. In other words, our mind drifts away from the words of the Prayer and instead hovers in mid-air…

What does it mean, to "undergo assaults by the enemy", and that "there is warfare"? It is because we are fighting the enemy and the enemy is retaliating. That alone, should encourage us to continue with the Prayer with even more perseverance, with more attention, and with more hope and divine consolation.

Of course, as we mentioned, what is required of us is willingness and patience. We must not daydream during the time of prayer, to the extent that it depends on us. On this point, the blessed Chrysostom roughly says the following: *"My good man, if you yourself don't listen to your prayer and don't pay attention to your own words, how can you demand - and with what naiveté and audacity - that God Himself listen to you?"*

Most certainly, struggle is imperative; and gradually –as we said- quality will come from quantity. After all, this also applies to all the other sectors of our life: the outcome of the quantity - of the many times that we persevere - will bring quality, as well as improvement. That is what we had to say about thoughts during the time of praying.

Praying can never be autonomized. We mustn't say the Prayer mechanically, lifelessly, like the motion of a clock… tick-tock, tick-tock… without digesting, without understanding what we're saying; rather, we should sense those words, we should fully sense the Prayer inside us.

Thus, to begin with, we should whisper the Prayer. And, if we put extra effort into it and dedicate more time – with the appropriate conscience (a contrite conscience, needless to stress) – if we put in more effort, both qualitative and quantitative, then, gradually, we will be able to say the Prayer more easily and noetically, with more ease; to say it inside us, with our mind. This is achieved by having repeated it many, many times. Besides, this is the reason we especially insist on this method of saying the Prayer - because it is succinct: "Lord, Jesus Christ, have mercy on me" and because the mind can concentrate far better and get used to these few words and as such, be able to repeat them without any exertion. Whereas, the assorted content of other prayers cannot be easily "assimilated" in order to be repeated in our mind automatically – the way that the Jesus Prayer can be.

We might also mention the following... (I don't think it's inappropriate to be taught by other things that we may observe in our lives). For example, when labourers work from day to night, they tend to repeat the words to a song, or hum a tune almost without meaning to, merely out of habit; well that repetition not only doesn't tire them, nor is it to the detriment of their performance at work, but on the contrary, it seems to actually relax them and comfort them and gives them a further boost, strength and courage in their labours. I believe you can understand what we mean by this example...

And if we persevere even more, without wearying or getting bored or giving up, and persisting in the Prayer at length each time, and at the same time apply all the instructions of the Church, then, in time, if God favours it, perhaps some might receive the gift of the noetic prayer of the heart. This means that those who do receive it, will be able to say the Jesus Prayer thereafter with their heart, without any effort or pressure; without the slightest effort any longer on their part.

We stress once again that we must not selectively do what we like – no matter how much we'd like to - just because we want everything made to measure to our own specifications (such is Protestantism), but instead, we should definitely observe complete obedience to everything that the Church commands, without exception.

Most certainly, the state created by the noetic Prayer (during which it automatically springs from within our heart without any exertion whatsoever and effort by us) is a gift of God. But we must not forget that God finally bestows His gifts only to His true strugglers – to His spiritually valiant fighters. Otherwise, if it wasn't done thus, it would have been an injustice on the part of God – something that is entirely unbefitting.

Those who haven't experienced what we just outlined shouldn't try -or exert themselves by trying- as they will not comprehend it in depth: i.e. that the heart, without any exertion whatsoever can, eventually, repeat the words of the Jesus Prayer automatically. The reason is because it is truly a mystery – a product of God's energy. Because, let's not fool ourselves, it cannot be learnt or gifted; it can only be achieved through experience and our personal struggles. No matter how hard we may listen, how hard we study, if we don't struggle properly, then regrettably, we won't achieve anything whatsoever.

We here, with our feeble powers, are simply giving certain simple guidelines, with the help of which we strive, not to teach of course but to exhort you, so that if possible we might all savour and become personally familiar with the inexhaustible mysteries of the Jesus Prayer. Thus, each one of us can finally understand accordingly, depending on one's own spiritual state.

Thus for example, if someone delivers a high school level lesson to a listener of Primary school level, then the listener will not understand anything beyond whatever is of Primary school level, because that is all that he has learnt. That is why we here are not trying to actually teach you this Prayer, but only trying to give you an incentive for the Prayer.

Correspondingly and analogously, even the word of the Gospel –as strange as what we shall say may seem- is not per se the revelation of God, as we may perhaps believe and imagine. Then what is it? Well, the Gospel is the word that tells us ABOUT God's revelation; because a revelation is, after all, a personal matter for each person – it is one's personal Pentecost.

To be even clearer, for example when Christ in the Gospel says *"I am the Light of the world"*, an entirely uninitiated person perceives it differently; a wavering believer perceives it differently, as do a lukewarm believer, a conscientious believer, a struggler… but perceived entirely differently by Saints like Gregory Palamas and Simeon the New Theologian.

Let's mention a characteristic example. When a University Professor no less (now deceased, albeit an otherwise good person) used to read excerpts from Saint Simeon the New Theologian who was describing his (humanly) indescribable divine love, he could not understand the Saint's words, nor could he imagine in the least to what heights man's grandeur can reach, inasmuch as he is able to partake of the glory of God.

But, even though Saint Simeon's words were all written in the Holy Spirit, to what did that professor attribute them – unfortunately, fatally, tragically? He attributed them to…. personal, psychological phenomena in Saint Simeon; that is, the Saint's experiences were supposedly attributed to his idiosyncrasy – to his personal psychosynthesis, we could say. As if that could ever be possible!!! Oh, the horror of it! Can you imagine? And to think that the professor was thoroughly praiseworthy in other matters; that is, he had every good intention, with an otherwise impressive range of works! Just imagine, if that professor were to read the part (I can't remember the words exactly) where Abba Isaac said: "*While in prayer, man is in control of his words, whereas when he has been swept up, into a "sighting" of God, a sighting of the divine Light, then all words and verses of prayers cease; that is, man ceases to pray. And not only is he not in control of the words of the Prayer, but man's very being is swept away, exclusively to where and for as long as the divine Light leads him. It is precisely this, beyond-the-mind, ineffable "sight" of God that surmounts every other prayer. Because it is only in this state, that the struggler –to his amazement– is able to "see" the truly Unobservable One. It is then that he can invisibly 'see' the truly invisible God."*

We could mention an incident here, where a certain "God-sighting" ascetic was afraid to raise his arms in a praying position and pray to God. What do you think he was afraid of? He was afraid he might be "raptured" up to a "sighting" of God without actually seeking this, in case he is "visited" by God and others see him "externally" with arms outstretched towards heaven, but because of his raptured state and his partaking of the divine, he himself would not be able to communicate with the environment around him.

Experience of the Uncreated Light.

But, we could also mention something inverse. One time, they told the Elder Paisios of a certain speaker who had spoken about the divine Light; about how beautiful it was, and how beautifully the speaker had spoken of it. To which the blessed Elder replied with sorrow: *"Yes, the speaker described it beautifully, undoubt-*

edly; except that he spoke of things that he himself was not familiar with, through experience."

Just imagine, my dear brethren, a very intelligent, capable, yet born blind person who has studied everything regarding the tangible light; who knows all the rules and the laws that govern natural light and who explains it all to us wonderfully, and in the end being confronted by the following question: "Mister speaker, everything you said was well and good, and perfectly expounded; but could you tell us if you yourself have personally ever seen the light that you described?" Well, he will be forced to reply: "Alas, I haven't ever seen it myself; I don't have that experience of light, because quite simply, I was born blind."

We mentioned all these things, if not to emulate them (which we should, with discernment), it should firstly be so that we humble ourselves deep down and not imagine that we are something special or that we have reached a certain spiritual height, and so that we don't cultivate personal self-delusions that lead us away from the path of our salvation. Because that is why Christ came to earth: to make us partakers –here and now– of His divine Grace. Christ didn't come, to merely make us better people externally, pietistically.

In that blessed state of the noetic Prayer, the heart on its own inexplicably and inscrutably repeats the Prayer –everywhere and continuously– regardless whether a person is performing manual labour or even a certain intellectual labour. For example, regardless if one is walking, talking, even if sleeping or working, or tackling a mathematical problem, or whatever labour requires our focused attention; if that person has the noetic Prayer firmly embedded in his heart, he is able (in parallel to whatever other labours he is preoccupied with) to repeat the Jesus Prayer, and always in the inexplicable manner as stressed earlier.

Besides, this is the truly blessed state that the Apostle Paul alludes to, when he says ***"pray without ceasing"*** (1 Thess.5:17) which he also gives us as an instruction, or, as mentioned in the Old Testament: ***"I sleep, but my heart is vigilant"*** (Song of Songs 5:2).

So, in essence, it is this state of the noetic prayer of the heart that the word of God alludes to and the Apostle Paul advises all Christians without exception – not just the monastics.

That, dear brethren, was all for today.

7. THE ADVANTAGES OF THE PRAYER

First of all, let me wish all of you, albeit belated, a Good and Blessed Lent, with a rich spiritual bounty for you all: with fasting – both in quality and quantity, because fasting is the beginning of every good thing. It is the first step; it strengthens our will; it is a way for man to "crucify" himself; his constitution is benefitted, because with fasting, a certain detoxing ensues, and, above all, we are being obedient to the guidelines of our holy Church and thus burying our self-centeredness. Because, my dear brethren, for man to fast, he must humble himself so that he fasts, not whenever he personally decides to, or for other reasons, but whenever and however our holy Church designates, and because it is precisely God's instruction.

But before proceeding to the continuation of the noetic prayer, we should complete our reply to a certain query, which among other things had asked if the fruits of the Jesus Prayer are obvious.

If you remember, we had said that as man progresses and fights on his spiritual front, then, analogously and accordingly, God allows – concedes – to each struggler's confronting even stronger opponents, more powerful, more insidious adversaries. Because of this, the struggler is not always able to directly perceive his progress. After all, the pure gain from that spiritual struggle is not so much the spiritual struggle per se; it is the genuine humility that arises from it. And man is not crowned for his virtues and his struggles; rather, he is crowned for that acquired humility, which is the product of his personal spiritual struggle and is acquired immediately after that personal struggle.

However, for humility to arrive, it is imperative – absolutely imperative – that he confront temptations. Without any struggles, you should know that humility is either impure or quite possibly that of novices; it is not the enriching humility of true strugglers. And without any temptations, you cannot become acquainted with your weaknesses, my fellow. You will always be ignorant, you won't know yourself; you will soar above the clouds, and will be in spiritual darkness. Without trials you cannot be actually humbled.

It is indeed a mystery. The more a person progresses spiritually – correctly, that is – the more he will see just how far behind he is. Even if he does see some improvement, then along with that improvement he will see even more clearly, more realistically, more properly, more pristinely, just how deficient he is. And that is precisely what gives him a boost for new spiritual decisions and spiritual struggles.

Whoever makes a certain spiritual attempt and with it, feels self-sufficient – that is, if he feels that it is adequate and he doesn't feel he needs something more – then he hasn't understood anything about the meaning of proper spiritual living; what genuine Orthodox spirituality is. He is unaware that perfection – even of those we are perfected – is never ending. As the Holy Fathers say: *"the never-ending perfecting of the perfected ones"*... a state that also extends into time-less eternity.

Of course the progress of the saved ones in the Kingdom of God - which will come after His awesome Second Coming – will occur effortlessly; that is, not like now, when one has to sacrifice their (spiritually understood) blood in order to make progress. Progress can now be attained only after spiritual sweating. Even the All-holy Mother Herself, Who surpasses even the Cherubim and the Seraphim in glory – and incomparably at that – at this very moment that we are talking, is even holier than She was yesterday. And She will be even holier tomorrow than She is today. Effortlessly, as we said. She will be holier than today, in the sense that She will be even more receptive of the divine Light, because quite simply the divine Light is not a reservoir that will one day be depleted.

Of course, to clarify this once and for all: the more that man progresses, the more he can discern how far behind he is. This new state has nothing to do with melancholy, disappointment and all related consequences; quite simply, the person in that state feels incomparably better than before, nevertheless, he has an underlying, beneficial and salvific unrest; a beneficial unrest that is incomparably beyond every kind of sobriety, every kind of calmness and every kind of peace. It is that beneficial unrest which prompts him to move on, to new spiritual exercises and new spiritual states, given that he can "see" new spiritual horizons opening before him.

According to the words of the holy Fathers, man feels an "insatiable satiety". In other words, while feeling "full", he still has the urge to press on, for new spiritual struggles. These are of course mysteries of the Holy Spirit and can be perceived only by those who are dedicated to spiritual struggles: that is, how can man feel full, yet at the same time feel the need to become even fuller – much, much fuller.

Don't see this as something strange, dear brethren. Human words, human verbal forms cannot adequately cover the phenomena of spiritual living. They cannot complete them, nor can they even vaguely approach them. If life around us and within us is shrouded by mystery – by general admission – then by comparison the spiritual phenomena are by far shrouded by an inexhaustible mystery, inasmuch as they spring from God and are directed at His logical creations when they seek Him.

Permit me at this point to add something more to the pertinent question which had asked if the person struggling with the Prayer can perceive his own personal progress.

To this, our reply is that at the beginning of the spiritual struggle, God condescends to approach us; and one of His ways of approaching us is by giving us some spiritual "sweet treats" in order to attract us, to sweeten us with His Grace; to draw us closer to Him and pull us away from sin. Sin, especially at the beginning, will deceive us. It appears to be sweet, regardless if sooner or later it will lead to an unimaginable bitterness, both in this life, but much more so in the eternal life. Thus, at the commencement of our spiritual turnabout, there will be moments when we can actually feel the presence of God. We can sense this whenever we make a certain spiritual turnabout: we are overwhelmed by a feeling of solemnity, an appetite, which to us may have previously been inexplicable.

However, eventually, over time, man also feels the withdrawal – the lifting – of Grace, depending of course on each case, because all the instances of spiritual states and of spiritual strugglers are innumerable and various. Of course at this moment we won't go into details. We will just mention here that if someone is interested, we would direct him to the Russian archimandrite Sophrony who authored the book titled "SAINT SILUAN THE ATHONITE" and anything else he may wish to study. In Patristic literature one can find how Grace is lifted, in examples of spiritual strugglers.

Thus, at some point onward, man begins to experience the withdrawal of the first-time Grace – the taking away of it. After which, he is forced to struggle with the passions that used to be buried inside him, and of which the struggler had (wrongly of course) imagined he was ridden, once and for all. This is why we should never, ever, feel reassured in our spiritual living, until our dying breath. As the wise Priest, Fr. Epiphanios Theodoropoulos used to say, "flesh-tomb" – that is, the passions of the flesh (and not only those) can only be ended by our tombstone. Until the tombstone is placed over us, there is the danger at any given moment for the passions to resurface, in one form or another.

So we repeat, that from a certain point onward, it seems as though Grace abandons the struggling person; however, in reality, that same Grace secretly gives that person the strength, the spiritual tolerance, the courage, to brave the various painful spiritual experiences. Because, if we were actually abandoned by divine Grace, then we would automatically fall into a void, as the blessed Elder Paisios used to say (and in fact when he was at an advanced age at the time), shortly before his death. What did he used to say? Listen to his words: *"If Grace deserts me, I will be the first to be found dancing in taverns, at parties, at music clubs."* Forgive me for saying things so simply, but that's exactly how the Elder used to express himself, with a charming laugh, in order to show that we owe everything to divine Grace.

But Grace never deserts man, unless he is permanently proud, or, unless we ourselves deliberately abandon Grace and generally abandon and put to disuse the various divine weapons which have been given to us for our spiritual struggles. Thus, even when man experiences the withdrawal of Grace and is tested and suffers, even then, Grace fortifies him, essentially, and in a mystical way…

Let's give a more vivid example. Remember Anthony the Great, who suffered demons for sixteen whole years… and with what temptations they had provoked him! Well, it was only after these trials that the divine Light had engulfed him, and he had asked Christ, Who had then appeared before him: *"Where were You, Lord?"* To which Christ had replied: *"I was next to you, Anthony, monitoring your struggles."*

That's what usually happens in spiritual matters. At first, the struggler savours a certain joy. But then, many trials will follow – depending of course on the receptiveness of the person and on the respective divine plan. So, joy at the beginning, followed afterwards by many trials. And if the person doesn't back away (this is where the valiant can be seen) – if he doesn't become disillusioned, but instead continues to struggle and suffer, ah, then will follow an incomparable, much greater spiritual joy.

My dear brethren, I want to believe that – even if they are only a few – there are some who have had at least a small taste of Grace. But I'm afraid that – if not all of us, almost all of us – do not afterwards display the necessary endurance for the spiritual trials that follow, nor persevere in the struggles as we should, thus depriving ourselves –alas– of the immense joy that follows, which, when it does come, surpasses in enjoyment, in quantity and quality, every other experience of this lifetime. This celestial joy is superior to every other enjoyment of this lifetime – whether that enjoyment is lawful or unlawful. Anything terrestrial, even the most praiseworthy, pales before the charm and the pleasure that is generated by this spiritual joy.

As Fr. Paisios used to say to us, in the beginning God gives us a tiny sweet, in order to draw us away from sin. But then He gives us the necessary tools so we can personally toil and make our own sweets – make our own "candy store"... turn ourselves into "confectioners". But that requires toiling. It requires personal labour on our part first of all. Or, as the same Elder used to say, even more characteristically: *"When you have a young sapling, a young plant, that plant in the beginning requires only watering, it needs only "pampering". But later, when it has gradually begun to grow into a tree, if you don't prune the plant, then no matter how much you water the tree, it won't make the necessary progress; that is, it won't produce the expected fruits."*

Well, that's about how it is in spiritual matters. For spiritual fruits to appear, spiritual pruning is necessary. Spiritual surgery will be needed. Saint Siluan the Athonite had an awesome visitation of divine Grace at the beginning – in fact he even "saw" Christ Himself in a divine Light. However, Grace afterwards departed from him (subjectively, of course), and then for many years he suffered the tortures of demonic offensives. He suffered continuously from thoughts: for example, at times his thoughts would tell him that he was a saint, and other times, that he would not be saved. Just imagine, while doing full body prostrations on the ground, he would see transformed demons in front of him, standing upright and mocking him... and all the time, he would have the bitter impression that with those prostrations he wasn't worshiping Christ, but the devil!

We of course don't have such instances – of seeing devils or anything of that sort... but, do you know what it is, my brother, to be worshiping God and feeling that instead of Christ, you are worshiping the devil? May this sort of thing never happen!

Pursuant to this, Saint Siluan said, "*If I hadn't received that initial, strong "dose" of Grace, I would not have lasted through that demonic torture a single night. But the Grace that I had received was so intense, sweet and determinative, that I was able to resist those innumerable macabre demonic nights, for many years.*" And elsewhere, in another context, Saint Siluan would say to Christ: *"Lord, I want to pray, but thoughts won't leave me alone."* Upon which, he heard a divine voice saying to him:

"That is how the arrogant suffer." Then he heard that famous (and familiar to all of you) phrase: *"Keep your mind in Hades, and do not despair"*. In other words, keep your mind contrite, and don't despair with the things that happen to you.

So much, dear brethren, as regards that query.

We have mentioned these things, because we consider them to be very basic and useful; because many of us, while we begin a certain struggle, afterwards, with the slightest excuse, we abandon it, ignoring the "games" that Grace plays. What can we do? We want Paradise there, and we also want it here? Constantly? It can't be like that. It takes hard work, to attain Paradise. What does Saint Isaac say? *"My brother, you wish to ascend to heaven and yet you take into account your labours, your pains and your sacrifices? Don't you see how other people act, for other, secular matters? Learn from them."*

And in this case also, my dear brethren, we must keep it well in mind that the Jesus Prayer requires a lot of work; it requires courage, it requires a lot of patience; it is not possible to acquire these things that we desire in one evening, two evenings, a month... Of course more important is the discarding of the old self – and that is what we should ask for, with our prayers. However that requires a lot of patience and a lot of work; I don't like to beautify things.... I want to be truthful.

Another query is the following: "Whether it is permissible to pray for those of other religions".

Due to limited time, we can reply epigrammatically: Of course it is recommended and imperative that we pray for those of other religions also. Let our personal prayer for them, with or without a prayer-rope, be for example: "Lord Jesus Christ. Have mercy on Your servant so-and-so, or Your servants so-and-so".

However, we shall analyze all these things further along. However, we cannot give the names of those people, or of heretics (that is, the non-Orthodox), to Priests in order to be commemorated during the Mysteries of our Church – the divine Liturgies, the Proskomide, etc. In other words, those names cannot by any means be commemorated in the Divine Liturgy.

That's all we had to point out, with regard to the queries that relate to our topic.

Now, let's recall that on the matter of the Jesus Prayer, in our previous meeting we had reached the third stage of the Prayer, where a person who is in that state can recite the Prayer, with his heart, no longer forcefully or with any human effort, whether he is working manually or even mentally – even while asleep. This state, we stress once again, is a gift of God. And

God gives His gifts whenever He sees fit, and whenever He wants to. But we must not forget that God gives His gifts only – and strictly only - to those who struggle, and in fact struggle properly.

One time, the newly-revealed Saint Siluan the Athonite was conversing with another struggler monk. The other monk said to Saint Siluan: "Everything is fine whenever I perform any manual labour; the Jesus Prayer can be repeated mentally while working and I am able to keep it steadfastly in my mind. However, when I need to do something that requires special attention – for example, if it is an intellectual labour – then I cannot simultaneously keep the Prayer in my mind because my mind is focused very intensely on that labour." This was what the monk had confessed to Saint Siluan. Then Saint Siluan smiled at him subtly, and with sorrow and love replied: "That doesn't happen to us..."

Those were the only words that he said. Of course he was implying that he himself had attained the Prayer - in other words, that, no matter what he was doing, he kept the uninterrupted Jesus Prayer within him as a gift of God – regardless if he was among the many workers (being hugely responsible - as the Monastery's steward if I remember correctly), in spite of the work, in spite of the many workers he directed, and in spite of the external vicissitudes that he often had to confront...

Let's insert a parenthesis at this point. I think most of you probably know it. It's about Fr. Fotios from Mytilene – a charming priest, presently well into his old age, who had officiated at the Monastery and had visited us on several occasions, and who had met (then Father, now Saint) Siluan.

Among other things, Fr. Fotios had narrated the following to us at the time:

It was when Fr. Fotios was still a young monk on the Holy Mountain. He had gone to the Russian Monastery of Saint Panteleimon at one time, where (then Fr.) Siluan lived as an ascetic. It was during that visit, that Father Fotios needed Father Siluan for a certain job that had to be done. He looked for him, but as he couldn't find him, he then went and knocked on the door of his cell, which was the natural thing to do. However, even though Saint Siluan happened to be sleeping at that time, he nevertheless got up straight away, and calmly and willingly assisted Father Fotios. In fact he even stayed with him for quite a while, because it had to do with a very serious project that demanded a lot of time. Father Fotios was very impressed by the willingness, the calm and the kindness displayed by Father Siluan. But, when he afterwards mentioned all these things with immense pleasure and instinctively to certain other monks that were also ascetics at the Russian Monastery - that is, after Fr. Fotios had taken leave of Fr. Siluan - that was when he was informed, that the moment he had been waking up Fr. Siluan, the latter had just gone back to his cell, minutes before, to rest after an all-night vigil! That made Fr. Fotios admire Fr. Siluan even more, for his gentle demeanour, and his secret, inner exercise – that is, because he didn't utter a single word of complaint such as "you know, I've just come back from an all-night vigil; wait a while", etc… Nothing of the sort. That was the kind of subtlety and discernment that were characteristic of Saint Siluan. He didn't say "You know, I just laid down to rest; If you like, come back later… I can't right now…" He not even hinted at anything like that. Such was the impression that was made on Fr. Fotios by Fr. Siluan's stance, that this incident remained in his mind for many years. Suffice it to say that he narrated it to us after almost 60 years, perhaps even more. He was a young monk at the time; he is an old man now, and yet he remembers it like it was yesterday or just a few moments ago.

Anyway, let's continue:

During his later years, Fr. Paisios had visited a certain monk who was on his deathbed. Out of extreme humility, that monk kept telling Fr. Paisios that he had spent an entire lifetime in futility and in sin. He kept saying: "*I am nothing but sin… I haven't done anything worthwhile.*" Then, to give him courage (because he knew of the monk's secret spiritual work), Fr. Paisios said to him: "*Let's not bother with those things – with the past. OK, so you didn't accom-*

plish anything; but now, when you're asleep brother, isn't the Prayer being repeated on its own?" To which the monk replied with his dying breath: *"Well, at least that is happening. Woe to me, if that weren't happening!"* In other words, he regarded as perfectly normal for the Prayer to be active on its own, during his sleep. Satisfied with that response, Fr. Paisios said to that monk, right before his end: *"Well, if that is happening, don't be afraid of your heavenward journey. Everything will be fine. God will save you."*

Forgive me, dear brethren, but now I recall other relative stories from the Holy Mountain. A similar incident comes to mind, which was also narrated to us by Fr. Paisios:

One time, there was a Romanian monk who was on his deathbed. He was the underling of a certain Elder and both were very old. When the underling was near his dying breath, a doctor who happened to be nearby went to see him. It was on a feast-day of the Holy Mother. The doctor's name was Daniel. He had gone there to offer the dying monk his last possible human services. But then in desperation the monk's Elder kept beseeching the doctor - in broken Greek, as he was Romanian, like we said: *"No, Danilo (Daniel), no do anything. Leave him... better to die today, because today very important day – it is Holy Mother Feast-day. Even if you do something, he will die tomorrow or after tomorrow. Better to die today, which is feast-day. Big blessing... Today is Holy Mother day..."*

Let's not comment here, on how we would handle similar situations…

This method of the Jesus Prayer has three main, major advantages:

First of all, there are no restrictions as to the place and time. That is, we don't need to have our own special space, a special room, books and any other equipment. We can say the Prayer everywhere and always, at any given time, whether we are undisturbed, or if we are preoccupied with other business in parallel and simultaneously. Even when we are travelling, or performing a chore, or when we are walking, or during work breaks… and at any hour and moment of the day, as already explained. In a nutshell, there is no unsuitable moment for the Jesus Prayer. It is always adviseable, always imperative. It is not merely allowed; it is imperative… it is always beneficial, always salvific - and instead of constantly thinking and listening to a whole lot of other things which, if not harmful are –to say the least- useless and futile; they disorient us, they blur our mind. So instead of doing that, we can offer to ourselves the Jesus Prayer, at least from time to time, in lieu of solid spiritual nourishment. That is the first, major advantage. There is no need for a special space, no need for special conditions.

The second major advantage that this form of prayer has is that there is no requirement for a particular, personal literary and philosophical training. There is no need for specific knowledge. Let's not hide the fact that the causes can be many: all of us are more or less deficient when it comes to theological-literary knowledge and because of it, we cannot understand the otherwise excellent, profound meanings of the Troparia hymns that are chanted in our holy Church during Her divine services. Because, for one to fully understand those excellent Troparia, they must also be familiar with the Old Testament, the New Testament, the lives of the Saints, the writings of the Saints, ecclesiastic history, dogmatics, and to also be familiarized with some ancient Greek. And quite often – as for example during Christmas, Theophany and certain other feast-days – they must be very well acquainted with ancient Greek.

These hymns should also be rendered properly by the cantors. As you can understand, for all the aforementioned things to manifest themselves simultaneously is not an easy achievement – not to mention that it is actually very difficult. Therefore it's quite natural to often feel somewhat bored during the services in church. Because, if one doesn't understand what he is listening to, then regardless if there is an excellent spiritual atmosphere thanks to the chanting, it is not strange for one to feel bored. Therefore, instead of having that frequent, not-so-salvific feeling precisely because we don't understand the meaning of what we hear, it is far more beneficial and useful, in parallel to the excellent spiritual clime created by the byzantine chanting, to repeat every now and then the Jesus Prayer to ourselves: "Lord Jesus Christ, have mercy on me".

Or, if we happen to hear a Troparion that pertains to the Holy Mother, we could repeat the words "Most Holy Mother, save me"; or, if a Troparion pertains to a Saint, we could repeat the words "O Saint of the Lord, mediate in my favour".

This action is far more useful, far more beneficial (than feeling bored).

However, beyond all this, if the major Saints of our Church – for example of the caliber of Saint Gregory Palamas – had found much greater spiritual repose and benefit in the Jesus Prayer rather than in the other, lengthier prayers or in Hymnology, all the more that we should prefer it, given that we lack the necessary theological and literary background as mentioned earlier.

Of course, in order to be more explicit so that there will be no misunderstanding, by general consensus, both change and variety appeal to our human nature. Otherwise, a form of spiritual stagnation is created in man. Therefore it is more relaxing, more natural, more beneficial and more productive, if we alternately chant internally or externally, and at other times say the Jesus Prayer, either in a whisper or mentally. The one doesn't conflict with the other. In fact, the one complements the other. That's how our human nature is. Everything that exists in our Church resides within the Holy Spirit. And, if we make use of all the aforementioned discerningly, our personal progress is maximized. After all, these things cannot be put into a mold.

For example, when we say a prayer or listen to a prayer in church – whether it's a chant, or whether it's one of the psalms of David, or whether it's something else, and if a certain specific verse of a prayer happens to strike us in a special way, if it "pierces" us, if it generates solemnity, if it "speaks" to us specially, then it is by no means a sin to loiter on that verse; in fact, that labour is both imperative and spiritually beneficial.

That's what the Holy Fathers say. Saint John of the Ladder stresses approximately the following : *"Don't lose this opportunity, because by means of that verse, by means of that contemplation, by means of that phenomenon, God has visited you so that your sins may be forgiven, so that you may be enlightened, and for many other reasons."* So you see, in Orthodoxy there are never any recipes, there are never any spiritual matrices. There is always discernment, which is the resultant of all the spiritual phenomena and all of the spiritual virtues. But let's not deviate further.

The third immense advantage that this Jesus Prayer has – which we had indirectly made reference to – is that the energy of this prayer remains unimpaired - we could say, even after the end of the Prayer. For example, when one says the prayer in a whisper (when he is alone that is), then, gradually and without perceiving it, when he finds himself in a public space the Prayer comes to him on its own, and he repeats it with his mind. In other words, the energy of the Prayer continues even after its completion.

These, my dear brethren, are the things we had to say in regard to the three major advantages that the Jesus Prayer has, versus the other, God-pleasing prayers.

Furthermore, apart from ourselves, it is recommended to pray – in the exact same manner always – for our entire family, for individuals to which we feel that we owe a certain debt of gratitude, for people who have a special need – a misadventure, a calamity, a certain illness, and generally speaking, for all of mankind and for all the living, by saying "Lord Jesus Christ, have mercy on us". The reason for this is because more than anything else, mankind suffers from a lack of prayer. And whatever we don't achieve most times with all sorts of teachings, extortions, arguments, threats, bargaining, discussions – which are never-ending and often wear us out and transfer us beyond place and time – we can achieve with the Jesus Prayer, because the Prayer hides a vast spiritual power inside it.

Thus, we can mention the names of certain very specific persons only once – at the beginning of the Prayer – and afterwards we can simply say as many times as we like "Lord Jesus

Christ, have mercy on us". That is, after having initially said "Lord Jesus Christ, have mercy on Your servants …, …, …, …. and all of mankind", we can thereafter simply say "Lord Jesus Christ, have mercy on us", where the "us" includes all of mankind, and additionally, in an entirely special and particular manner, all of the names that we had mentioned during the beginning of the Prayer. In other words, we don't need to burden ourselves with countless names and repeat them continuously, because that scatters our spiritual attention and moreover, it is neither feasible nor possible to remember all the individual names that we had initially deposited in the Prayer. That is why we can additionally say in closing: "*…and on those who have charged us, the unworthy ones, to pray on their behalf*". God knows for whom we want to pray, who we should be commemorating, and the ones that we have forgotten because of our weakness.

So, let's allow God to direct that humble prayer of ours, to wherever there is need, to wherever it must be directed, to wherever it is His will. In other words, let's simply say "Lord Jesus Christ, have mercy on us" – unworthily of course – and then simply let God act for us.

That was all for today.

8.
THE PRAYER FOR THE LIVING AND THE DECEASED

After extending our wishes for the remainder of the blessed Lenten season dear brethren, let's remember that during our previous synaxis we had completed the Jesus Prayer for all the living, with the words "Lord, Jesus Christ, have mercy on us."

Today, we are purposely stressing once again that, in order to pray for certain people using the Prayer, we don't have to exert and dizzy ourselves by continuously repeating their names. It is enough to mention the names of those persons once, the first time, then we can continue the Prayer by simply saying "Lord, Jesus Christ, have mercy on us" – without repeating the names over and over again, given that the word "us" embraces the names of all mankind – and, in an entirely singular and special way, the names also of the living that we mentioned during the first recital of the Prayer.

At this point, we are reminded of an incident when we were still laymen and on our way to the Holy Mountain, when we met someone on the ship, who had told us the following: "Well, if you're going to the Elder Paisios, tell him to pray for me. I am Narcissus. The Elder will understand. He knows my case". After a few days, I had gone to see the Elder, but when I finally arrived at the Elder's hut, I had totally forgotten the name of the man who had asked me to convey his supplication for prayer, so I said to the Elder Paisios: "Elder, someone told me to ask you to pray for him. He knows you and you know him. Forgive me, but I have just forgotten his name, because it is quite a rare name". To which, Fr. Paisios replied: "So what? So you forgot it. God knows the name; God knows who that man is. I will pray for that individual, and God already knows what problem he has".

However before we move on and discuss the Jesus Prayer addressed to those who are reposed, let's say a few words to begin with, in regard to the prayer rope, given that we were publicly asked about it.

The prayer rope may not be compulsory during the Jesus Prayer, but in the end, it is a very practical item and very useful, and as such, is definitely a must. In other words, the Prayer is far more effective when it is repeated with the help of the prayer rope – when we are undistracted.

First of all, the prayer rope itself is a blessed article, given that it has a Cross hanging from its circumference. Then, each of its knots is composed of nine crosses. Tradition has it, that this cluster of Crosses in each knot was discovered so that the devil cannot approach the prayer rope, because the devil is terrified whenever he spots the sign of the Cross. As in the case of a certain monk, who, when knotting Crosses so he could count his prayers, the devil would unravel the knots afterwards.

Now, the primary use of the prayer rope is to give us a steady and automatic rhythm – a steady frequency when reciting the Prayer. We might mention at this point that the rate is: count one knot, say one prayer; not say one prayer and bypass several knots. Unfortunately, this phenomenon has been observed, perhaps on account of a bad habit – that is, when one says the Prayer once, and skips over the knots in twos or threes or tens. That is not appropriate, and besides, it doesn't make any sense.

We repeat: we must not repeat the Prayer mechanically and in haste; we should instead fully "digest" the meaning of the words that we utter; for example when we approach a high-ranking person with a request, not only are we careful what we will say, but also how we will say it. Well that applies to an even greater degree when it pertains to the heavenly King, the King of kings, our Lord Jesus Christ.

So, on the one hand we must fully digest the words of the Prayer and we thus not only don't become tired, but we actually become relaxed by the words of the Prayer. We furthermore maximize a personal benefit, which is the outcome of the Prayer. But on the other hand, we must not allow pauses from prayer to prayer, so that our nous/mind won't have time to remain suspended and think of other things, and especially to become scattered, especially when we are the beginning of this spiritual exercise of the Prayer.

Furthermore, as regards inhaling and exhaling during the Prayer, or from prayer to prayer and more generally during the various techniques of concentration – such as seated on a stool – we must have a certain body stance, for example with our head lowered towards our chest etc.. Without snubbing all these things, we do however think – at this point at least – that it is expedient to not mention them on a general level. And the reason for this is because we are afraid there may be misconstruals and each of these things becomes an end in itself. Because the final aim and fruit of our prayer must be the lifelong discarding of the old self and a God-inspired humility.

You see, these technical methods – especially the technique of breathing – demand a proper guide, as there are many latent dangers that are not only spiritual but also organic. That is, the person praying may come to believe that he has reached a certain level, that is, an advanced one; in fact to the degree that he may reach the point of delusion. Delusions during the times of prayer, when the healthy personal, inner spiritual background is absent are not few, nor are they easily distinguishable.

Let's give a simple example: Imagine a novice who has "fallen head first" (excuse the expression) into the exercise of the Prayer and keeps reciting the Prayer incessantly, and out of excessive zeal doesn't even stop to say "good day" to anyone who passes by him for fear he will supposedly lose the coherence of the Prayer; if that person doesn't become reasonable, but persists in that same attitude and continues saying the Prayer and disregards those who pass by him, well, nobody can foresee what serious problems or spiritual and organic nature he may acquire.

But, aside from the aforementioned dangers, the main reason we don't refer to the various techniques is because we unshakeably believe that these techniques in the long run play a very small role in the fruition of the Prayer. This is because almost all of the weight falls on our correct spiritual struggle. For example, whoever says the Jesus Prayer and comes into "contract" with Jesus – not to be forgiven, not to be corrected, humbled and enlightened – but instead says the Prayer in order to acquire certain spiritual charismas, for example to brag about "possessing the Prayer", well, then God (again out of love) will not give him the charismas he anticipates, so that he won't become boastful.

Let's read what a certain Russian Starets (Elder) has to say on the subject. He says: *"We should leave the transformation of the focused, verbal prayer into a noetic prayer and a cardiac prayer. God will undoubtedly transform it, if He sees us even slightly matured and cleansed, through the application of His commandments"*.

And he continues, further along: *"He who is still in an infantile stage in his spiritual development is not suitable for spiritual gifts. He will not use them for the glory of God, nor for his own benefit, or for the benefit of his fellow man".*

Then he goes on to say: *"On the contrary, he will use those gifts and harm himself. He will become arrogant, and will become boastful, full of fatal self-importance and a destructive disregard for his neighbor. And if - albeit lacking any charismas but instead having a whole pile of weaknesses - we nevertheless act boastfully and humiliate the other, can you imagine what would happen if we were entrusted with a spiritual treasure, or special charismas? Wouldn't that become the cause for yet another, worse catastrophe for us?"*

As Fr. Paisios used to say to us: *"God wants to give us a bit of Grace, and yet, no sooner has He given it, we are immediately overcome by pride, we think we have become important, and so, for our own benefit, He doesn't give it at all. My dear fellow, you're boasting about Grace? The* (original, Greek word – charis-charisma*) –etymologically- implies that it is a "gift", that it is something which God gives to you; it doesn't imply that God is certainly bound to give it to you".*

And in another context Fr. Paisios used to say on the same subject that quite often, man resembles a young child or an infant, which strives to climb up a huge ladder; and, although it is on the first rung, it struggles to climb up to the second one but isn't able to. It tries, but falls…

it gets up, but falls again… This continues over and over again, until its mother picks it up because she feels sorry for it, and immediately places it on the top rung of the ladder… following which, the child says to itself 'Ah! Well done! I made it to the top!'" Well, if a person thinks the way that we just mentioned, then he thinks even more immaturely than that infant.

So, getting back to our subject, the first advantage of the prayer rope is the steady rhythm it offers. Of course if we wish to go deeper into the matter of frequency –which to us is of extreme importance - it would be good to mention the following:

If each and every person struggles for a length of time with the spiritual exercise of the Jesus Prayer, at a certain point he will attain –let's call it– "his own particular frequency" of the Prayer, (that is, of that particular period). This happens to also be the frequency with which the person says the Prayer, when the Prayer is repeated on its own, spontaneously, effortlessly, noetically, in the heart.

For example, when the praying person is asleep, or when he awakes and realizes that the Prayer is being repeated on its own inside him, well, that is precisely the recommended "particular frequency" for the Prayer to be recited by that person, at any given time. Thus, in our humble opinion, we believe that we have a spiritual coordination from within us, by which the benefits of the Prayer are maximized.

Then, a second, huge help that the prayer rope offers is that it reminds us to say the Prayer when our mind drifts here and there, back and forth etc. In other words, it is somehow a perfect annotator, as it constantly reminds us to say the Prayer. Because as you can understand, if you are holding a prayer rope in your hand, then, even if you stray a little – and we definitely stray every now and then – then when you look at the prayer rope, it will remind you of your sacred and incessant duty. That's why it is such a good thing to hold the prayer rope in our hand whenever that's feasible, and never part from it. And if we do part from it, may it be only out of an uncontrollable spiritual joy and pleasure – the way it happened to a certain soul, who would cease the Prayer and abandon the prayer rope because she had become spellbound. And whenever she became overwhelmed by the excess of divine pleasure and the supernatural divine radiance, the prolonged time that she had spent praying in that state would seem far too little to her. Or, more accurately, it seemed as though Time had stood still, given that she was in a state of empirical sensing of the immaterial God. But for experiences like that, and even superior, more beautiful and enchanting ones, a great deal of proper effort is necessary.

At this point – and because we all become disillusioned more or less by our mind's inability to concentrate – I will read you, my dear brethren, an excerpt from Saint John Chrysostom.

Says the sacred Father: *"The remembrance of the name of Jesus incites the enemy for battle; a soul that pressures itself to say the Jesus Prayer can, with that same prayer, find anything – both the good and the evil. The soul can first see the evil in the depths of its heart – that is, it can locate it– and then it can see the good. This prayer can prompt the serpent into action, and it can likewise crush it afterwards. This prayer can dig out the sin that lives nested inside us, and that same prayer can uproot it and ostracize it."* And the blessed Chrysostom concludes by saying: *"It takes a lot of time and effort to evict the enemy and for Christ to settle within us."*

Now on the matter of difficulties during the Prayer: well, above everything, God observes the predisposition in a person. It is only human at times – out of weariness and negligence, or perhaps out of a certain turmoil of the soul or other causes – to notice certain side effects which aren't of course praiseworthy. However, even then, it is by far better to say the Prayer rather than to not even attempt to say it.

Fr. Paisios used to tell us on this point: *"Look, a secular person came to me in a hurry today and he was scandalized because he had been to a certain monastery and had seen a monk there who was laughing. So I began to berate him, and said to him: 'Look here! That monk first of all is the sacristan of the Monastery (Elder Paisios knew him); which means, he remains inside the church almost all day. The daily services last around eight hours; beyond the eight hours the sacristan needs three to four hours to prepare the oil lamps, the ceiling lights and all the other preparations that are foreseen for all daily services. So, it's only natural for him to not remain all those long hours inside the church as unmoving as a column.' Then I also said to him: 'Are you aware of the kind of effort that monk has to put in, and you, poor fellow, were scandalized with him? And what is it exactly that you do? You go to church for a quarter or half an hour, and only on Sunday… that's assuming you do go, and how you go, and why you go… then for the rest of the week, what is it that you do? Where do you go? Where do you frequent?... but, let's not continue along this line... And so, you became scandalized, just because he laughed a bit, or because he was tired and took a short nap inside the church etc.? Let me tell you, that his was a blessed nap, inside the Ark of the Church. God doesn't judge along those lines. Let's not act like the Catholics, who go to church for a short while and sit motionless there, like guilty cats or icebergs. We Orthodox feel like we're at home in church, and we are seated more comfortably, more naturally and more humanly'."*

The third, additional help that the prayer rope provides is that it is a very good counter; that is, we can actually count the number of prayers in our penance – the number of prayers that we actually recite – and as we know, there are prayer ropes with 33 knots, 50 knots, 100 knots, 300 knots and with 12.

Of course the 12-knot and 33-knot ropes are handier for one to have when in a public space (so that he won't be perceived and thus provoke)...

Then there are the "crossed prayers" that can accompany the prayer rope. In these cases, we hold the prayer rope in our left hand if we want, and with that left hand – count the prayers, knot by knot, as we say them. Then, with the right hand and in parallel with each Jesus Prayer that we say, we make the sign of the Cross (we sign ourselves with the Cross) and at the same time bow our head very slightly, that is, perform a light, mini-prostration as it is called. However, this move must be relaxed, so that the flow of the Prayer won't be interrupted.

Semantically however, it is appropriate that during every crossed prayer that we do, when we reach the words "have mercy on me" our right hand should be at the lowermost point of our prostration bow.

Of course these rope prayers can be plied, whether we are standing or kneeling. These prayer ropes, together with full-body prostrations, comprise the so-called "personal spiritual struggle" of monks – but not only of monks; they can also be observed by laypeople. These are considered far more drastic than the simple rope prayers, which are said freely, without any crossed prostrations. These so-called "free" prayer ropes can be plied, whether we are standing, or walking, or kneeling, or seated – or even if we are laying in bed, depending of course on the circumstances; whereas, as already mentioned, the crossed prayer ropes are plied when we are mainly standing; and when there is a special reason, an excessive weariness, then they can be plied while kneeling.

The prayer rope can also be plied during "full-body prostrations"; in other words, from the standing position that we are in, we drop to the floor on our knees, supported by our hands, and we bend down until our head almost touches the floor. In parallel to this move, we make the sign of the Cross with our right hand, and with the prayer rope in our left hand, we count the prostrations that we make.

It is recommended during prostrations – without this being compulsory of course – to say the Prayer more analytically, that is, "Lord Jesus Christ, Son of God, have mercy on me the sinner". This of course is a purely personal choice. In our opinion it is better to say the words of the full version of this Prayer, which will give us enough time to perform the complete prostration – that is, from the standing position to fall on our knees and then bending down until our head is almost face down towards the floor, then getting back up to the standing position. Consequently there must be enough time in order to accomplish this. Thus, by saying more words with every prayer, we will have enough time to go through the moves more naturally, more comfortably, more harmoniously. Even so, we need to ensure that when we say "have mercy on me the sinner" –and because it is appropriate semantically- when saying the words "the sinner" our head should be in a lower position, that is, it should almost be touching the floor. That way, with the full-body prostration, we vividly display – we indicate – our fall, because of our personal sin before God. So much, on the subject of prayer ropes.

Of course we need to stress once again that we who are in the world -and with so many various obligations- need to practice saying the prayer in a whisper or mentally, in our mind, and without a prayer rope; that is, when occupied with other jobs and most of the time it is not possible or appropriate for us to simultaneously keep up the Prayer along with the prayer rope.

Whatever the case in the matter of the prayer rope, what is important is that we should not provoke the others. We must not make a show of ourselves in public. At the same time however, we must have a godly zeal for the confession of our faith, for the Prayer etc.. And naturally these things are a matter of discernment, and can never be cast into a mold.

At this point we might also mention something about the deceased – that is, how the Jesus Prayer is applied to those of our brethren over time who are asleep in Christ. We had been asked the following by Fr. Paisios – in our student years at the time: "What is more useful, more necessary - to pray for the living, or for the deceased?" And we had replied, perhaps sentimentally: "For the living, so that they may repent". To which the wise Elder pointed out to us: *"It is preferable that we pray for the deceased, because they can no longer do anything to help themselves like the living, who are able to repent by themselves"*. Thus, it is imperative even more so to pray with the method of the Jesus Prayer for the deceased, by saying in their case: "Lord Jesus Christ, repose Thy servants".

I would like you to make sure that you never write the word "dead" on the note listing the names that have to be read "for the souls of...", or refer to them as dead in our conversations, because quite simply, for Orthodoxy, dead people don't exist, as a Common Resurrection of all the deceased is anticipated. Those who are reposed can no longer do anything to help themselves, because for them, the time limit for repentance has expired. However, the most benevolent and most righteous Judge, God, wants to save everyone, even at the last moment. That is why He expects us to do something for this.

And here we have a very delicate point, in which we can see God's noble mindset. Unfortunately, however, instead of being moved and humbled and enchanted by His noble stance, it often scandalizes us and disorients us. In the present instance, if God were to intervene on His own to save those souls of the deceased, He would essentially be violating their freedom of choice – that is, our freedom in general – our self-government, which is the most precious thing that we have. Because there is no logical being that lacks freedom. And inversely, every free creature is, from its creation, by definition a logical being.

And the second major difference between us and the logic-less animals, is not strength (there are animals far stronger and far weaker than us), nor is it intelligence. But let's not digress to this detail. The greatest difference between us is our freedom and logic. To make it even clearer: No animal, no matter how strong it may be, will ever consider changing the natural environment which it inhabits. Whereas people, as we all know, are capable of turning everything upside down, and making everything unrecognizable. But God Himself, in His overall plan for the salvation of man, has respected man's freedom and has acted so that it is not violated, even in the least. Because we have been created with freedom and He insists on keeping us free-willed. Of course the fact that we are suffering the consequences of our free will is another matter altogether.

One time, we had asked the blessed Elder Paisios: "Why didn't Christ become incarnate earlier, to have ensured the certainty of salvation for more people?".

He replied: *"He wanted to, but couldn't find the suitable person as His "vessel". He eventually found the spotless, All-Holy Virgin, who had willingly accepted the Annunciation by the Archangel Gabriel."* As we all know, following Her wisely inspired hesitation, She had said the famous words *"**Behold, the handmaiden of the Lord; may it be so, according to your word**"*. After these words by our Most Holy Mother, God became man, to make us gods by Grace.

Or, to generalize it somewhat: Why doesn't God perform any provocative miracles in our day and age? That is, why were there so many miracles during the first years of Christianity, whereas later the multitude of miracles decreased? The reasons are many: faith, the predisposition to struggle, and many other reasons. But the chief reason is because God respects our freedom. In the past, during the beginning of the spread of Christianity, there was a need for many miracles. For example there was a need for the speaking in tongues ("glossolalia") on the Day of the Pentecost. It's not because the miracle per se was of any special worth; rather, it was because of the miracle, that it was easier for people to believe in the teaching of the Holy Apostles and all the other workers of the Gospel during that time, who, with the miracles that they wrought, all became more credible and more acceptable to their audiences. But, if those miracles – which were innumerable – had also continued at the same frequency afterwards, then man's freedom would essentially have been annulled, because the continuous miracle essentially abolishes faith and creates a form of compulsion.

So, with regard to the deceased, God expects from us to freely offer our self-government, our freedom, voluntarily, out of a sense of honour, for the sake of the souls of the deceased, so that God can find a cause (if we can use that term) to help the souls of all those deceased.

That way, everyone benefits – both those who are saved and those who are condemned, given that in both states there are infinite, unending gradations. In Paradise - that is, "in the house of the Lord" as the Scripture says – "there are many mansions". There are many states of the saved ones, depending on how much they had struggled while on earth. Exactly as in Paradise, the same applies for Hell, where there are likewise various gradations. You see, my dear brethren, even in Paradise there are the so-called spiritual "circles".

What I want us to recognize at this point is that when man leaves this life, his soul departs from his material body. The soul goes to the appropriate "place", where it has a foretaste of either Hell or Paradise. However, even in Paradise there is not a complete or final state, given that the resurrected bodies of the saved people aren't there. The Common Resurrection of the reposed has not taken place yet. With the exception of the Most Holy Mother and the God-Man and firstborn Brother of ours, Jesus Christ, all of the Saints are in Heaven, but only as souls.

And when the Lord had said that blasphemy against the Holy Spirit (which, as we had explained during another synaxis, is the lack of repentance) will not be forgiven – not now, nor in the age to come - the wise interpreters explain that Christ had meant that the age to come was the period of time which commences from the personal, terrestrial death of each individual and extends to the Second Coming of Christ. That is when the Kingdom of God will have finally and fully arrived. Therefore, according to the aforementioned words of Christ, it is understood that up until the moment of the Second Coming, the other sins can be forgiven, through the prayers of the militant Church – that is, through the prayers of us all, for the souls of our departed brethren.

And so, along with the "thrice-holy" prayers, the memorial services, and the names that we give to be read in commemoration during the Proskomide, as well as during the 40-day liturgies and the charities for the souls of the departed, in parallel with everything that our holy mother Church has established by divine inspiration, it is recommended and imperative that we recite the Prayer "Lord Jesus Christ, repose Thy servants". As for the other things pertaining to the reposed, dear brethren, God willing we shall continue with a further analysis during our next meeting.

9.
THE METHOD OF THE PRAYER WHEN ADDRESSED TO THE HOLY MOTHER, TO THE SAINTS, AND FOR THE DECEASED

In our previous meeting my beloved in-Christ brethren, we had talked about the Prayer for our reposed brethren, with the words: "Lord Jesus Christ, repose Thy servants" and had mentioned that this prayer is recommended and compulsory even more for the reposed, as compared to our living brethren, given that the reposed can no longer be of any help to themselves, because the deadline for their repentance has expired.

And let's just stress once again to your love that only during the first time – when we begin reciting the Prayer – it is very good and is recommended that we mention several names of reposed ones – relatives, acquaintances, or persons towards which we feel a certain spiritual or material gratitude, and the like... That is, we should state those names only during the first recitation of the Prayer, and then, without tiring or dizzying ourselves –thus confusing our mind by repeating the same names over and over again every time we recite the Prayer- we can simply say "Lord Jesus Christ, repose Thy servants". In those words, "repose Thy servants", all of our reposed brethren throughout time are included; but in an entirely distinct, unique and particular way, also included are the names that we commemorated during the first recitation of the Prayer. That way, everyone benefits – both the saved and the condemned – since there are infinite gradations in both states.

In the Gerontikon (the Book of Elders) there is the following incident with Abba Makarios: *"Said the Abba Makarios: While walking in the desert one time, I found a human skull discarded on the ground. When I nudged it with my cane, the skull spoke to me. So I asked it, 'Who were you?' The skull replied 'I was the priest of the idols and the gentiles that used to live in this place. And you are Makarios, who has the Holy Spirit in him. When you commiserate with all those who are in hell, Makarios, and you pray for them, they find some consolation.' So I asked the skull, 'What is the consolation? And what is hell?' And the skull replied: 'As far as the sky is from the earth, that's how big the fire below us is. And we stand inside that fire, from foot to head, and we can't look at anyone face to face; instead, we stand with our back stuck against another's back.' A complete lack of communion, that is. And the skull continued, 'So, whenever you pray for us, Makarios, one can see the other's face somewhat. That's our consolation.' And I wept after this and said 'Woe to the day that man was born!' Then I said to the skull, 'Is there a worse kind of torture?' The skull said to me, 'The bigger torment is below us.' So I asked it, 'And who are the ones there? The skull replied, 'not having known God, we find some mercy. But those who had known Him and denied Him and did not obey His will, are all below us.' In other words, they were in a much worse situation. So I then took the skull and buried it."*

That, my dear brethren, was what Abba Makarios had narrated to us.

As Fr. Paisios had also told us regarding this matter, *"It's not the same thing, finding yourself in a dark and hot prison and suffering in there but not being able to see anything, or being in the same prison and every now and then being able to have a cool refreshment."*

You can surely grasp what the Elder meant.... A spiritual refreshment.

Of course, we have the rare cases of people having exited that hell, but not that their position had simply improved, while they were in there. The same improvement applies for those who are in Paradise; however we also have cases where their souls had been transferred from hell itself, and placed in Paradise.

For example there is a mention in Patristic Literature of the case of Saint Gregory Dialogus – a major Saint who lived in the West – who, after intense and prolonged praying, had removed the soul of a renowned Roman emperor called Trajanus from that hell.

In closing everything that we had to say about praying for the reposed with the particular method of the Jesus Prayer, we should pray for all the reposed throughout time, without exception, except of course for the already recognized Saints of our Church. We should include everyone on our list of names for commemoration, because even those who are spiritually rich become richer with our prayers.

Even if there is the certainty –so to speak- in the conscience of the Church that certain souls have immense outspokenness with God, we need to unhesitatingly commemorate them during Liturgies, if they have not been recognized officially as Saints -this is the proper order of the Church- and we should generally pray for their souls.

Because, as your very familiar Fr. Paisios the Hagiorite used to say, *"if you give a multi-millionaire one, two, a hundred, a thousand more drachmas, not only are you not harming him, but are actually making him richer"*. You understand... But if we see this in a positive, God-pleasing "wiliness", from the moment that the one who we are praying for really does have outspokenness with God, well, he in turn will pray for us for an additional reason, and as such, from this aspect we will have an additional spiritual benefit.

And so, with the "Lord Jesus Christ, repose Thy servants" we can pray for the souls of all the reposed.

At this point let's move on and analyze to your love the way in which we must analogously and respectively pray with the same method, to our Most Holy Mother.

For Christ we say "Lord Jesus Christ, have mercy on me", "Lord Jesus Christ, have mercy on us", "Lord Jesus Christ, repose Thy servants". Now let's see what we can say – analogously as always – to the Most Holy Theotokos. But before embarking on that topic, let's say a few introductory things which are necessary.

Dear brethren, if Christ as a man is the ontological mediator between humankind and the Holy Trinity – that is, if the Incarnation per se is the cause for God's favour towards the human race, given that Christ, as a man, had pleased the Holy Trinity to a perfect degree - it was because through Christ that we have become reconciled with the holy and glorious Triune God, which had naturally been fulfilled during the event of the Ascension, when our human nature as a whole had risen to that height of the Holy Trinity. The consequence of that reconciliation and compromise was the sending forth once again of the energy of the Holy Spirit.

Well, then the Most Holy Theotokos is the most perfect moral mediator to the Triune God. The Holy Mother's outspokenness is immense. Suffice it to imagine that Her God, as a human, simultaneously is (and will always be) Her Son. As a Troparion hymn says, the Theotokos is the "cause for everyone's deification". That is why, in parallel to the prayers to our Christ, it is recommended and imperative that we also recite the "Most Holy Theotokos, save me" for ourselves, and the "Most Holy Theotokos, save us" when we pray for all the living, as we have already explained.

Finally, we should mention the "Most Holy Theotokos, repose Your servants" for all our deceased brethren throughout the ages – that is, with the exact same method, either with the prayer rope, or without it, as mentioned analytically for the prayers to our Lord Jesus Christ respectively.

Of course, as we said, only Christ is the ontological mediator Who saves; and that when we say "Most Holy Theotokos, save me, or save us" etc., it implies "mediate for our sake". As such, it has the significance of mediation. Quite simply, because the Holy Mother's mediation has an entirely special place in our holy Church – that is, relative to that of the other Saints – which is why honorarily, worthily, justly and appropriately for our Most Holy Mother, it is recommended that it is better to say "Most Holy Theotokos, save us", whereas for all the other Saints we should say "Saints of God, mediate for us".

To get an idea of the grandeur of the Most Holy Mother's outspokenness, suffice it to refer in brief and without historical details to the holy icon of the Holy Mother named "Paramythia" (Consolation), which is found in the Sacred Monastery of Vatopedion of the Holy Mountain. It was out of this icon that the Holy Mother had spoken miraculously, with a forewarning to the monks residing there to take certain safety measures because they were going to be attacked by pirates. Then something amazing happened: almost simultaneously, the Child Christ in that icon raised His hand in order to close the Holy Mother's mouth, saying: "Do not protect these monks. They are not worthy of their mission". Then the Holy Mother in turn took hold of Christ's hand to restrain Him from covering Her mouth. Ever since that miracle, the icon remained miraculously imprinted with the details of that incident, and not with the pose that had originally been designed by the hagiographer. Ever since that incident, most tonsures are customarily performed in front of that icon of the Most Holy Theotokos.

So much for the Theotokos, as regards the way in which we should pray to Her with the method of the Jesus Prayer.

Finally, apart from our Holy Mother – as mentioned earlier – it is to our benefit to pray, always with analogy, to the Saints on their feast day, by saying "Saints of God, mediate for me". Because each day is not dedicated to the memory of just the one or two Saints that are mentioned in the Calendar, or the many more Saints whose names are commemorated by the Reader at Matins, from the Book of Saints, in the morning.

Many more Saints are commemorated each day – Saints who are perhaps unknown to us but in God's eyes are Saints – who were reposed on that day. There are also other, local Saints who aren't recorded in the Books of Saints. And there are very many other Saints whom we may not know, but they know us, so it is to our spiritual benefit to invoke their mediations also.

It was when I was a layperson, during a conversation with the Elder Paisios with regard to the Saints, that I had felt the proximity of the Saints for the first time. This occurred on account of the content and the spontaneity of the Elder's words. Then, in my naivete, I instinctively, conclusively said to the Elder: "You mean, Elder, that all the Saints know me well...". And the Elder replied, jokingly albeit saddened: *"Then you should give them your phone number and address so that they can also contact you!"*

With this comment, the Elder probably wanted to say that our Saints may know us, but that we have to do something so that they can "contact" us – or, rather, so they can help us. In other words, we must give them a cause for them to help us – and the Saints will always help us. That is, our stance, our way of life and our conscience must be such that will allow the Saints to help us.

In the summer of 1979, Fr. Paisios changed his abode for the last time. He changed Cell at the time, and departed from the Cell of the Precious Cross located at Kapsala, to his last Cell at Panagouda. In the past, a certain major Russian ascetic called Father Tychon had lived in the Cell of the Precious Cross for a number of years, who had tonsured Fr.Paisios to a Great Schema monk. When the blessed Elder Paisios departed from there and moved into the Cell at Panagouda, during his first night there he was exhausted (as was natural) and –apart from that- he had all his books still in boxes because of the move. So, during that first night, when reciting by heart the Evening Service and reaching the part where he had to read from the book the Kontakion prayer to the Saint of that day, he obviously didn't try to find the Menaion (the official book with saints' feast-days), but instead said "Saint of God –whoever you are – mediate for me"...

He said it quite spontaneously, simply, but with sincere faith. And right then the commemorated Saint of the day (it was the 3rd of June) appeared to him and introduced himself! However, because of his exhaustion, the Elder Paisios didn't catch the Saint's name clearly when he introduced himself. So the Elder Paisios asked him after the self-introduction: "*Who are you? Saint Lucian*?"

"*No*", replied the Saint, "*I am Saint Lucilian*" (because there is both a Saint Lucian and a Saint Lucilian). After that incident, the Elder affixed an ordinary paper icon of Saint Lucilian in the tiny chapel inside his Cell, in remembrance of that Saint's visitation that day.

One other time, the same Elder also told us of a certain monk, who very frequently saw the main commemorated Saint of each day.

These were just a few points, dear brethren, regarding the prayer to the Saints of each day. And may we add that this prayer can be recited either with or without the prayer rope. When we are in church and Troparia hymns are being chanted to a certain Saint, we can say "Saint of God, mediate for me" in parallel with the hymns.

We can additionally mention here that, if one wishes to, he can (apart from the "Saint of God, mediate for me") also say "Saint of God, mediate for us", depending on the circumstances and how it springs from within him; or, he can even pray to the Saints for the souls of the departed also.

Now, after all the above, let's mention that the most appropriate analogy of time we should spend with the prayer rope – for all of the prayers that we mentioned earlier – is as follows:

Without of course being absolute, we are simply expressing a thought - on the basis of course of what we have heard from our Elders:

Three units of time dedicated to Christ, crossing ourselves, and one unit of time to the Holy Mother, crossing ourselves.

Then there can be three more units of time for Christ, with the Prayer, (which can be "free": without compulsory crossing or prostrations or stances), and likewise one unit of time for the Holy Mother, "free".

Also, three units of time for Christ, with the words: "Lord Jesus Christ have mercy on us" for all the living, and one unit of time for the Holy Mother, saying: "Most Holy Theotokos, save us".

Also, three units of time for Christ, saying "Lord Jesus Christ, repose Thy servants" and one unit of time for the Most Holy Theotokos, repose Thy servants".

And finally, one unit of time for the Saints of each day.

Now, the remaining time we can (and it is recommended) mainly say "Lord Jesus Christ, have mercy on me", either with the prayer rope or without it, or in parallel with other activities as explained earlier on.

Now, the "three units of time" can pertain to either three 300-knot prayer ropes, or three 100-knot prayer ropes, or even ropes of another number. Thus, if -for example- the "three units of time" are with 300-knot ropes, well then, as you can understand, the "one unit of time" would mean one third of the 300; that is, one hundred knots. If the "three units of time" are with 100-knot ropes, then the "one unit of time" would mean about thirty-three knots. In the second case (of 100-knot ropes), the routine would work out to seventeen 100-knots: 4x4=16 and 16+1 (to the Saints). Whereas if the prayer ropes are 300-knot ones (the typical ones vary), that would mean seventeen 300-knot prayers. As the great ascetic monk, Fr. Ephraim of Katounakia (Holy Mountain) would tell us, he used to ply seventeen 300-knots during the night.

Let's say a few related and pertinent things at this point, which he had told us. His words were the result of his own personal acquired experience, because Fr. Ephraim was a model of suffering and struggling obedience. He used to say: *"Without obedience, the Jesus Prayer will not come. You can recite the Prayer for as long as you like, but if you don't have obedience, the Prayer will not come to fruition inside you."* He also said to a monk: *"If you wander aimlessly about here and there, you won't be able to say the Prayer the way you should. You will be forcing yourself and it won't respond. You will be forcing yourself excessively, without the analogous result. If you're a "wanderer" – that's how he called it – "it won't flow"... imagine this expression for the Prayer! Whereas, if you go somewhere, not by choice, but out of obedience to your Elder, then, wherever you go, even if there are certain dangers or external disturbances or crowds etc., you will see that by being in obedience (and of course provided you pay attention, to the degree that you can), there will be instances where the Prayer will spring forth from within you with greater ease, even greater than when you were in the stillness of your Cell". And that -naturally- is a gift of God, because of your obedience."*

My dear brethren, spiritual living is indeed a very subtle thing. It is the science of sciences, the art of arts. Quite often, a correct thought, a correct inner stance of ours, can become the generative cause for the Prayer to come in our sleep, or to facilitate the Prayer during our waking hours. On the contrary, a bad thought, an incorrect stance, even if in a suspicious or latent form, hidden inside us, can unfortunately become a spiritual barrier which minimizes the supply, the fluidity, the ease of the Prayer. It becomes an inhibiting factor for the Prayer. That's why a certain Elder used to say: "Sometimes, one correct thought can be worth more than a thousand prostrations".

We could also mention at this point that, if we want to (and of course with the advice of our spiritual father), we can recite the prayers of certain Services, especially if it's not possible to go to church, or for some reason we don't have the appropriate conditions or the relative books that are necessary etc. Thus, we can recite those Services with the prayer rope, either by reciting the Prayer vocally, or mentally, with or without the prayer rope, accordingly, depending on if the Service is Vespers, or Matins, or the Evening Prayers or the Prayer preceding Holy Communion, or the Supplication to our Holy Mother, or other Services.

Of course we wouldn't want to get into details today, at least during this phase, but, as a first update, we could mention that the time more or less demanded for a specific Service that we wish to recite with the prayer rope should be segmented -approximately of course- into: a Prayer to Christ, a Prayer to the Holy Mother and a Prayer to the Saint or the Saints commemorated on that day.

For example, if an everyday Vespers Service lasts about half an hour, we can dedicate (more or less) twenty minutes of the Prayer to Christ: "Lord Jesus Christ, have mercy on me"; about five minutes to the Most Holy Theotokos, saying "Most Holy Theotokos, save me/save us", and about five minutes to the Saints commemorated on that day.

Of course these things can't be forced into a mold; in essence, it is a personal matter for each person and a topic that he has to take up with his spiritual father. The rubrics are very many. Everything is good and holy, as long as they are done with the proper disposition.

In fact, Fr. Ephraim of the Katounakia used to say on this matter: "When you ply the Prayer on your own, the entire benefit is clean – it is yours, so to speak..." That's how he used to express himself... "Whereas, if there are many others present around you, inevitably something or other will happen, and sooner or later a certain disruption will result". Of course the Elder was probably referring to himself; for us, things are not exactly like that. In our case, both the one and the other are needed – that is, both the common prayer as well as in private.

We might mention something additional at this point – that, with this method of the Jesus Prayer – whether with a prayer rope or without it – it is recommended and imperative that we also say other kinds of prayers, whether they are supplications or glorifications etc. For example, we can say "Holy Trinity, our God, have mercy and save us". We can say it with or without a prayer rope, or we can also pray to our holy guardian angel- or even to all the bodiless holy angels, especially on every Monday, when, as we know, all the celestial powers are honoured.

We can also pray to the Cross of Christ, as it possesses an indestructible power; we can say "O Cross of Christ, save us by your power".

It is further beneficial to pray to All Saints, by saying "All Saints, mediate for me or us", depending on the case.

And of course it is imperative that we pray to the Saint whose name we bear.

So, we can see that the instances where we can say many other prayers with or without the prayer rope are very many.

Several years ago on the Holy Mountain, there was a monk who truly exerted himself ascetically and who, while plying his prayer rope and saying the Prayer during a Monastery's night vigil, had seen the Archangel Michael in a vision, looking exactly like the icon of his that was in that same Monastery. He saw him wearing a mantle that moved. Now, who do you think that monk was praying to at that moment? He was praying to All Saints; and yet, the Archangel Michael had appeared in a vision. Well, this is possible also, given that the entire celestial world is governed by the common energy of the one and only Holy Spirit. This works in reverse also; that is, the one and only Holy Spirit acts analogously and variously, as He deems fit.

And we might mention here that the aforementioned monk – who, by the way, had an extremely mellifluous voice – when chanting one day had become so carried away by the sweetness of his melody, that his mind got caught up by the meanings of the words of the Troparia he was chanting. God then allowed his inner, spiritual eyes to open, and what do you think he saw? He saw the devil dancing beneath the chandelier, mocking and taunting him. He went into such a severe spiritual shock, that he barely managed to finish the Troparion he was chanting. He has since regarded himself the plaything of demons, and albeit having an extremely mellifluous voice as we said, with great difficulty would consent to chant again.

Now, in closing, let's mention that whenever possible, it is preferable that we prepare ourselves before embarking on the Prayer. It is very beneficial, if some elementary study precedes the Prayer, because that helps our mind to concentrate on the Prayer much better. The reminder of death will help us a lot, so that our Prayer might be purer and more focused – that is, without any distractions and hoverings. And generally speaking, anything that helps our concentration and improves our personal performance in the continuous labour of the Prayer is truly blessed. Whereas reversely, whatever distracts and obstructs us we must, if possible, and at any cost discard.

A certain monk for example used to cover his eyes with his hood when reciting the Prayer, so that he wouldn't receive any external impressions that would distract the focus of his mind.

Of course the cases are innumerable, and dependent on the conditions and the personal idiosyncrasies of each individual. What is of importance, however, is that we create a suitable clime in p s sreparation for the Prayer.

These, dear brethren, were the things we wanted to mention to your love, with regard to the Prayer. If necessary, we shall revert on the topic in the future.

But let us never forget that the Prayer cannot, in the end, be taught, just as all spiritual matters deep down cannot be taught. They are all learnt through personal experience.

The Prayer can never be wasted; however, it is for this reason that the cunning one seeks to find ways to hinder us from saying the Prayer. He always lays in waiting, in one form or another, and tries to distract our attention so that we end up not praying, or praying the least possible and incorrectly. Because quite simply, apart from the spiritual benefits that we attain through it, the Prayer also freaks out the demons.

The blessed Elder Paisios used to say on this point: "*Very often the cunning one would send me visitors, not for any benefit, but in order to distract me from the Prayer. But the reverse also occurs: I can perceive when those who visit me have been sent by God".*

My beloved brethren, it is my wish that, just as a young child – an infant – cannot perceive what milk consists of but can sense that it is being nourished by it, and thus fervently and tearfully yearns for it and suckles it, likewise we, always with an infant conscience, should suckle on the energies of the Prayer within us. Because there are many who have written whole books on the Prayer – and they are right to do so, from one aspect – but what is most important for us, is who, finally, is sweetened and savours the unending fruits of the Prayer. But for that to be attained, as we have said, struggle is required.

So then, struggle... Struggle, my brethren, struggle. Because what the world needs today is, after all, the existence of saintly souls. And that which a gracious and sanctified soul is worth and can accomplish, is not possible for all the rest, no matter how hard they try. Because unfortunately in our day and age (it appears that the problem is a general one), we the contemporary Orthodox as a rule seem to be placing our efforts in the external organization of our lives etc., and not attending as much as we should to our personal sanctification – when both these things are necessary. And, first and foremost, our personal sanctification is imperative. All the other things that preoccupy us should after all be conducive only to our personal spiritual progress. If we worked on our inner self, we would eventually save ourselves and would also lure many others towards salvation. We however do the exact opposite: before dealing with our own self, we seek to save others, so that not only do we not benefit, but the others for obvious reasons are inclined to resent us and are scandalized.

These were the things my beloved brethren that I had to offer to your love.

It is my wish, therefore, that we all acquaint ourselves with this method of prayer that we analyzed, because, as we said, although it may be the simplest form, it is nevertheless the most drastic method of prayer for confronting our three major enemies: our selves, the devil and the world, so that we might victoriously enter the Kingdom of Heaven by the Grace of God.

Amen! May it be so!

Archimandrite Arsenios Katerelos
Abbott of the Sacred Monastery
of Saint Nicholas Divrys, Fthiotis Province.

«UNIA: THE FACE AND THE DISGUISE»

THE BOOK BY FR. GEORGE METALLINOS NOW CIRCULATING IN ENGLISH

In this very notable essay, Father George examines the historical course and the significance of the religious-political entity named "Unia", that is, of the Papist communities in the Orthodox regions of Eastern Europe and the Middle East – mainly during the past four centuries – who have acknowledged primacy and infallibility in the person of the Pope of Rome. The author analyzes Unia's early link to the Papist "Holy Inquisition", but also to the Jesuits, who had originally organized Unia as a disguised Latinism. The strengthening of Unia was nothing short of the continuance of the Papacy's medieval struggle for dominance, for the implementation also of political and not only ecclesiastic authority by Rome. The Vatican's persistence in preserving and strengthening Unia despite the reactions of the Orthodox but also of many important Papist personages, proves that Unia continues to this day to be extremely precious to the Vatican, for the salvaging of its crumbled moral status and also for the weakening of Orthodox peoples, States and alliances. The matter of Unia is no longer a hiero-canonical one; it is primarily an ecclesiological problem and should be considered as a reason for the revision and redefinition of the theological dialogue of the Orthodox with an uncompromising and aggressive Rome. The text is also flanked by significant, related, pan-Orthodox documents.

book size (in cm): 12,5X20.5
ISBN: 978-618-81489-1-8
1st edition: 2015

Pages: 124
Language: English
12 Euro

GREEK ORTHODOX BOOKS

Liti GR – 57200
Thessaloniki, Greece
Tel. 0030.6907364372,
Fax 0030.2394072744

www.greekorthodoxboox.com

www.greekorthodoxboox.com

« NICK MARVEL AND THE WAR WITH THE BEAST»

If you have grown weary of the morbid clime of magic and occultism in children's spectacles and literature…

NICK MARVEL whose adventures will give you an entirely new dimension to what is nowadays considered to be a story for children.

Imagination in children's literature does not always have to be a bridge linking to magic and occultism – a phenomenon that is all too frequent in our day and age. Nor does it have to be an escape from a "tough" and "unbearable" reality. Imagination can be an opportunity for discovery, knowledge and adventure, within a healthy, enter-tai- ning and pleasant environment. Nicholas Maravelias, an average, modern youngster, lives within the reality, the adventure and the miracle of… life. By having apposed his optimism and his hope for personal progress to God's Providence, the certain love of his family – but also without shirking any personal effort – every moment of Nick's day brims with intriguing experiences. A veritable adventure. Nicholas Maravelias – to his friends and fellow students " Nick Marvel " on account of his liveliness, his patience and his good nature – has no need for "magic" in order to live intensely, honestly and responsibly. His is a life filled with marvels!

A series of books for "children" between the ages of 9 and... 99!
From Athens and Moscow to Essex and Constantinople: an exciting and adventure-packed journey, whose only unchanging element is Faith !

book size (in cm): 14X21
ISBN: 978-618-81489-2-5
1st edition: 2015

Pages: 218
Language: English
15 Euro